IDAHO
RIVER T

by
JOHN GARREN

Selway River
Middle Fork of the Salmon River
Main Salmon River
Lower Salmon River
Hells Canyon of the Snake River

**A guide to touring Idaho's most popular
wilderness whitewater rivers.**

**Garren Publishing
5450 S.W. Erickson Ave. A222
Beaverton, OR 97005**

To
Patrick E. Murphy

Idaho River Tours
Copyright © John Garren, 1987
Printed in the United States of America — 1991
ISBN No. 0-941887-00-6
Library of Congress Catalog Number 87-80296
Revised edition printed 2008

Cover photos: Greg Smith

CONTENTS

Acknowledgment

In preparing river logs for my first book, **Oregon River Tours**, it became evident that logging is a two-person job. Trying to log rivers in a kayak is particularly frustrating. All the river tours were logged in a raft using two persons. The second person in this duo is Mary Alice Thompson. She handles trip logistics, meals, a Volkswagen Bus and has personally logged each of these tours.

Mary Alice is a competent river person in her own right. She has a knowledge of river hydraulics that surpasses most boat persons and can confidently run class four rivers, except possibly at high discharge where strength rather than skill might be a factor. She is clearly the outfitter for these tours and a major contributor to the book.

Jon S. Garren and Jeff Garren are excellent paddlers and boating companions. They shared these trips by helping with photography and the routine chores inherent with any river trip. Most important they have a sense for guiding and safety. They are river wise in everything from dislocated shoulders to class five rapids. I can think of no two better paddlers to have around.

Typography by Pamela Martin.

Foreword

Within the central section of Idaho lies the largest classified Wilderness area in the contiguous United States. The Eastern border of this section is bounded by the rugged continental divide. Hells Canyon, the deepest gorge on the North American Continent, on the Western Idaho border is a natural geographic barrier. The North and Southern regions of Idaho also have formidable obstructions to intrusion. Idaho itself has a population less than Denver, Colorado. Special wilderness designations and government ownership of land all contribute in part to make this a remote area.

In spite of the Region's remote geographical location, knowledge and development progressed about this area with the Lewis and Clark expedition. Shortly after their traverse over the Lolo Pass, others quickly followed. Individuals were floating the Salmon River not many years after the 1805 Lewis and Clark expedition. By the early 1900's boating of rivers such as the Salmon was well recognized. Most of these early records of boating central Idaho were related to exploitation of natural resources such as mining rather than recreational boating as we know it today. It wasn't until after World War II that people seriously started to develop these rivers as a commercial recreational resource. This has resulted in the five most popular river tours in Idaho being nationally recognized as the Selway, Middle Fork of the Salmon, Main Salmon, Lower Salmon and Hells Canyon of the Snake Rivers.

Knowledgeable boaters realize that there are somewhere near twenty other Idaho rivers offering a wide variety of whitewater opportunities. Most of these rivers are essentially day trips although rivers such as the Bruneau or South Fork of the Salmon Rivers are overnight tours also. The Payette receives wide use, and the Boise River in downtown Boise, Idaho, although not a whitewater tour, is considered the "tubing" capital of the world. The Murtaugh section of the Snake is considered one of the best big water runs around, and the North Fork of the Payette is a nationally recognized expert run. It is not the intent of this book to list all of the river sections in Idaho that are best explored by the individual. Half of the nine best overnight wilderness whitewater tours in the lower United States are in Idaho, and they are included in this book. For the whitewater enthusiast, Idaho offers some of the best whitewater anywhere.

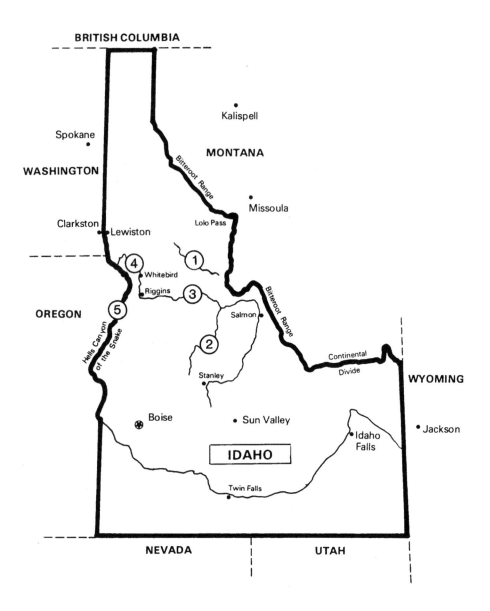

IDAHO RIVER TOURS

1. SELWAY RIVER

2. MIDDLE FORK OF THE SALMON RIVER

3. MAIN SALMON RIVER

4. LOWER SALMON RIVER

5. HELLS CANYON OF THE SNAKE RIVER

River Data

The intent of this book is to provide useful information primarily for the boater using these river tours for the first time or those who may use the river only infrequently. Each tour includes a river map, a trip narrative, a river discharge curve, and a river log with campsites and rapids.

Essentially this is a river log for the person who will actually boat the river. The log is believed to be unique because it is a graphical log including both time and distance.

In preparing the river tours, a certain research technique and river data gathering method was necessary. The most important data is discussed for the boater's information.

River Slope

River slope is usually measured by boaters in feet of river drop per mile. This data can roughly be scaled from conventional U.S. Geological Survey Contour Maps, obtained from river-mile index publications, or more accurately from river profile maps. By looking at the profile you can tell whether a river has a relatively constant slope or is what boaters call a "pool and drop" river. The latter will have more rapids which form at each "drop" section. The river slope is one measure of river difficulty. Steep river slopes will have high river velocity and will usually, but not necessarily, have difficult rapids. The river slope given in the log is for the trip average. This is an indicator of river difficulty but other factors must be considered when evaluating the river. When river profiles are available, it is good practice to review them in making an evaluation of river difficulty.

River Roughness

River roughness greatly influences river difficulty. The rocky "rough" stream channel provides the basis for a wide variety of stream hydraulics that form rapids. Hydrologists can determine numerical values for stream roughness, but a minimum of common sense experience quickly tells the boater whether the river is rough or smooth.

A relatively uniform stream slope and smooth channel usually provide easy river boating. A rough channel combined with certain river slope and discharge often ends up with names like TAPPAN FALLS, BIG MALLARD, SNOW HOLE, WILD SHEEP and WOLF CREEK rapids.

River Discharge

River discharge is one of the most important factors to be considered by the boater. There is a relatively narrow range of discharge that gives desirable boating for any river. Below some minimum value the stream velocity decreases, the rocks (stream roughness) become more troublesome, and the trip is difficult. The other end of the range is flood stage.

Fortunately for the boater, governmental agencies maintain a large system of stream gages on almost all major rivers. The river tours are referenced to a specific river gage along with recommended discharges. An effort has been made to select gages that are representative of the river and where the data is readily available daily, including forecasting, through a river forecasting center.

River discharge curves are given for each tour. This is a trip planning aid that will tell the boater the approximate river discharge during times of the year based on historical record. Actual discharge and short-term predictions can be obtained from river forecasting centers whose telephone numbers are given with each tour.

The terms low, moderate and high are often referred to for river discharge. A look at the discharge curve will quickly tell what discharge approximates these general terms which are also sometimes used to define risk.

Estimating Time of River Discharge

The river log gives recommended ranges of discharge for drift boating. These are general boating guidelines based on experience and judgment. Boating at discharges outside this range is tolerable under certain conditions, and the experienced boater realizes the lower discharges mean slow velocity along with rock problems. The top range of discharge means more powerful river hydraulics close to flood stage.

Usually it is desirable for the boater to schedule trips for the most probable boating periods between selected ranges of discharge. As an aid in predicting river discharge time, river gages were selected for analysis that typically represent river conditions. Sample data was plotted for the average monthly discharge over a discrete period of record. The resulting data gives a smooth graph based on past river history.

Plotting the average values gives a more useful graph than those based on one year's data. These graphs prepared for each river are considered sufficiently accurate for all long-range planning. As the trip approaches the boater should verify reality by calling the River

Forecast Center for exact data and short-term predictions of less than one month.

These curves are a practical means of estimating what periods of the year are normally used for boating within a selected range of discharges.

The River Log

The river log is the heart of each tour. Although boaters experienced in running a particular river often do not use a log, it is considered essential for boaters running a river for the first time. Rivers were logged by time which is then correlated with map data, river mile indexes and other information that can be confirmed. Much of the information shown on maps cannot be seen or identified by the boater from the river. Map contours and routine geography tend to blur on the river.

In this publication of **Idaho River Tours**, the time log has been combined with a map for easy reference. Most of the things shown on the map and time log can be seen from the river. Some things cannot be seen such as some airstrips, ranches or hot springs. The boater may want to know where these features are for emergencies or hiking to points of interest. By following the log, and with a little luck, the boater should not miss an assigned camp or stumble onto a major rapids unexpectedly.

Distance and Time

Distance is a difficult concept for most people while on the river. A new boater can get lost unless he has some check points as a reference. This is why time in addition to distance is included in the log. To say that the next major rapids is downstream 7.3 miles has little meaning, unless it is related to something familiar such as time. I have checked the logs frequently and find the time very accurate under similar conditions. When the times do vary, it is easy to re-set your watch at some convenient check point and get back on schedule.

The main concerns of most boaters are major rapids and camps. These are specially pointed out in the log. Generally, the boater should be prepared to scout and possibly portage major rapids.

River Mileage

River mileage conventionally starts at the mouth and increases upstream. Left or right bank is facing downstream. All the river logs use this convention.

Relative Drift Time

The relative drift time for various boats is significantly different. Log times are recorded for a particular type boat at a particular river stage. For the same type boat and reasonably similar river stage there is little difference in time. For example, it will usually not be necessary to correct times, except at check points, for canoes or kayaks, but if you are using a raft and the log time is for a canoe, you may expect the raft drift time to be longer by a direct ratio of 1.6/1.1 or about 1.5. Multiply the canoe log times by this amount and correct the log times before starting the trip. You should then come very close to actual times, and correct only at convenient check points.

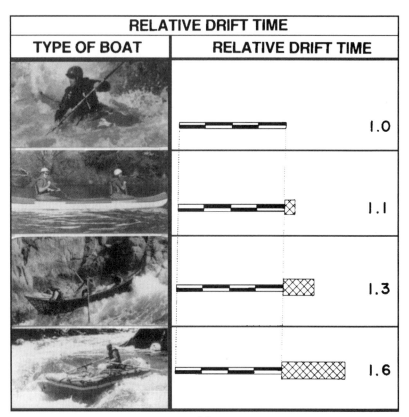

RELATIVE DRIFT TIME	
TYPE OF BOAT	**RELATIVE DRIFT TIME**
	1.0
	1.1
	1.3
	1.6

The river log trip time is actual drift time on the river. When you stop or want to get out for awhile, note the time; then when you start again, set your watch back to the time you got out, and you are back on the correct log time.

There will be some minor differences between individuals for rowing and paddling. The recorded log times are for drifting, which means paddling or rowing just to maintain position — or to maneuver with continuous but leisurely rowing or paddling in low velocity or slack-water areas. Log times might be cut in half in an all-out race, but the times are remarkably close for drifting.

River Velocity

One other main factor, in addition to type of boat, that influences drift time is river velocity. Within reasonable limits of river discharge from that shown in the log, it will be unnecessary to correct river drift time. If, however, the log is for 5,000 c.f.s. and you plan to boat at 2,000 c.f.s., it may be desirable to correct for the change in river velocity in addition to boat type.

Boaters are aware that as river discharge increases so does the river velocity. Yet even with the wide range of boats and river discharges used in these logs, there is a surprisingly narrow range of drift speeds, usually between 4 to 5 miles per hour for the trip average. Apparently as the river slows down boaters work harder at paddling, and as river velocity increases they maneuver and paddle approximately at river velocity. Canoeists, for example, can paddle between 3 and 6 miles per hour, and this variation partially compensates for river velocity changes.

Many boaters dislike a watch on river trips, yet it is essential if the boater is concerned about navigating on the river. I use time as a means of navigating in an attempt to estimate when river hazards will arrive and in order to avoid cooking in the dark or spending an unforeseen day on the river.

ESTIMATED RIVER VELOCITY

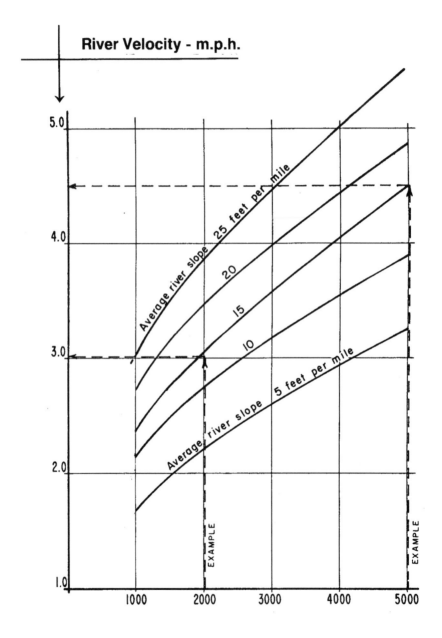

RIVER DISCHARGE — Cubic Feet per Second

FIGURE 2

Example: The log you intend to use was prepared for a trip with an average river drop of 15 feet per mile, using a McKenzie drift boat and at a river discharge of 5,000 cubic feet per second. You plan to use a raft at a river discharge of 2,000 cubic feet per second. From the Relative Drift Table (Figure 1) and Estimated River Velocity (Figure 2) graphs, estimate your drift time.

Time correction (boat type correction) (river velocity correction)

$$\frac{1.6 \times 4.5}{1.3 \times 3.0} = 1.8$$

It will take you about 1.8 times longer than the times shown in the log. This is a significant change, and you may wish to correct river log times to major rapids and special geographic check points before starting your trip.

Campsites

All of these river tours except the Lower Salmon are permit rivers, and some knowledge of camps is essential. The Middle Fork of the Salmon River has reserved camps that are a part of the river permit. There is usually some competition for the better camps, as knowledgeable boaters negotiate for the most desirable. The Main Salmon, Hells Canyon of the Snake, the Selway and the Lower Salmon do not assign camps or require a camp reservation. It is first-come first-served.

Hells Canyon of the Snake River has the most severe camp conflicts since many other recreationists in addition to float boaters use this river. Hikers, horse packers and power boaters all compete with floaters for campsites. Power boaters ply the full "Wild and Scenic" section of the Snake and do not hesitate to assert their rights to camps, sometimes setting up bogus camps or exchanging camps. Float boaters on the Snake have user limitations while power boaters do not. Very few float boaters can take a trip on the Snake and maintain a neutrality on the power boat issue. Power boats are also allowed on the Main and Lower Salmon Rivers. There is only one launch per day on the Selway so there are plenty of campsites. Camp conflicts or the chances of seeing another river party are remote. Campsite consideration has become a necessary part of trip planning and the camps shown with each tour should be a starting point. Campsites are subject to change as new facilities are added or new camps developed. The river managing agency can give up-to-date information at time of launch.

River Safety

River running is a risk sport, but contrary to popular belief, actual whitewater fatalities are surprisingly low. Reducing accidents or fatalities to a common denominator, such as drownings per 100,000 user days, the risk falls below other more acceptable sports. Sometimes water related accidents are not in fact whitewater accidents, and agency reporting methods may account for some of the discrepancy in facts. In any event rational people who boat whitewater attempt to reduce risk to the lowest practical level.

In order to advance skills and experience challenge, many boaters, by preference, boat near their skill limits. Logic might suggest that according to popular belief the majority of whitewater fatalities are poorly equipped beginners without any skill or judgment. There are no statistics to bear this out, and the risks of the novice boating Class 2 rapids may be very close to the risks of the expert boater attempting Class 5 rapids. Some boaters, by choice, are willing to accept greater risks than others. There is no criteria to determine whether beginners or experts are greater risk takers. There is a tendency to forget that all boaters were at one time beginners. If there are more accidents among beginning boaters than experts, it is probably because there are so many more of them.

The three primary factors influencing safety are equipment, skills and judgment. The boater has the control of and responsibility for each of these factors. No person, agency, certification or set of regulations can relieve the boater from this responsibility. The individual must make the decision whether his skills and the particular circumstances warrant running a river or rapids.

A high level of river skills and judgment only comes from experience. This experience develops people that are worth seeking out as boating companions since they are the only persons available for rescue and help. The river has a way of weeding out the frivolous who are unwilling or unable to develop the skills and judgment required of whitewater boating. River safety is strictly up to the individual and his immediate boating companions.

Rapids Difficulty Classification

Whitewater rapids are formed by river hydraulics from a combination of slope, stream roughness and flow. The most used and best understood method of classifying rapids is the international system based on a scale of 1 through 6 where 1 is the easiest and 6 the most difficult. Experienced river runners have classified major rapids on many popular river runs. The classifiers have developed a consensus on rating, and seldom will experienced boaters differ by one whole classification number.

The primary differences that occasionally exist in rapids classification often relate to confusing rapids difficulty classifications with boater skills. Although the two are related, rapids difficulty classification for a specific set of conditions is constant and independent of river or location. Boater skills and perception of rapids are constantly changing. Rivers are routinely being run today that were considered hazardous ten years ago. In most cases it isn't the rapids that have changed but rather the equipment, skills and attitudes of the boater. The Boater has the responsibility to confirm rapids classifications for himself, since it is the boater who will ultimately run these rapids. It must be emphasized that any rapids rating must also be associated with a river flow since rapids may change with flow.

To distinguish between rapids class and boater skills, it is best to use the numerical classification for rapids and an adjective for skills such as novice, intermediate or expert. Environmental conditions such as temperature, remoteness or ease of rescue may influence the judgment used in running a river, but these factors are independent of the rapids classification.

The western rapids classification system has been used on some of the southwestern rivers. The original scale was 10 with 10+ and 10++. This is double the international scale, making conversions between western and international scales easy. Other methods of rapids classification have been proposed, but they have not received any preference over the international classification by the boating community.

Different organizations have also used descriptions for each numerical classification. Many of these are lengthy and often reflect regionalization or a particular boating background. A simpler method that does not change the classification scale refers each classification to whitewater hazard varying from virtually no hazard to extreme hazard. The threshold of hazard for most boaters is Class 3. Obviously, boaters can have accidents in Class 1 rapids or no rapids at all but in terms of whitewater, hazards increase with the numerical classification.

Ordinarily river logs and maps only show Class 3 and greater rapids and named Class 2 rapids. In **Idaho River Tours** Class 1 rapids are not shown, but all rapids commonly accepted as Class 2 are shown. Obviously, some of these rapids "wash out" or may increase in magnitude with different flows.

International Rapids

Difficulty Class	Whitewater Hazard	Boater Skill
1	Virtually None	Beginner
2	Hardly Any	Novice
3	Threshold of Hazard	Intermediate
4	Moderate	Expert
5	High	Advanced Expert
6	Substantial Hazard to Life	None

Comparing River Difficulty

Many boaters who are boating a river for the first time would like to have some method of comparing river difficulty. Except in a general way this comparison has not previously existed. This can be particularly difficult for someone from a different region or anyone unfamiliar with the river in question. Since each river is unique, there is no absolute method of comparison, but there are factors the boater may consider in developing a judgmental comparison.

The river log that shows both the magnitude and frequency of rapids is the best information for developing a comprehension of difficulty since rapids are the primary measure of river difficulty. A log also defines the river section, which can be important since different sections may have varying degrees of difficulty. A formal method of comparing river difficulty is to consider the number and class of rapids, then reduce the number to a common denominator such as rapids per mile so that a 47-mile Selway trip may be compared with a 97-mile Middle Fork of the Salmon River trip. That has been done for the tours in this book.

River managing agencies, in an attempt to predetermine boater skills, sometimes require that boaters have experience in running rivers of similar difficulty. The agencies may or may not name rivers of equal difficulty. This sometimes forces boaters who have not run these rivers into a fabrication in order to comply with the regulation. Since rivers have not formally been classified and there is no uniform recognized method to determine skills, then only the boater can correctly assume the responsibility of deciding whether his skills are adequate for a particular set of river conditions.

Much of the data presented in this book is factual and may be confirmed by the boater. Other information such as rapids difficulty ratings or skill is judgmental and for the boater's use at his discretion.

River	Trip Length	Gage Height or Discharge	Average Slope	Mean Rapids Class	Class and Number of Rapids			
					2	3	4	5
Selway	47	Paradise Gage 2.0 feet	28	2.4	53	22	7	0
M.F. Salmon	97	M.F. Lodge Gage 2,500	28	2.4	88	32	7	0
Main Salmon Corn Creek — Vinegar Creek	79	Corn Creek Gage 6,000	12	2.3	44	16	1	0
Lower Salmon Whitebird — Confluence	54	Whitebird Gage 6,000	10	2.4	38	20	1	0
Snake Hells Canyon Dam Pittsburg Landing	32	Hells Canyon Dam 12,000	10	2.6	21	13	2	2

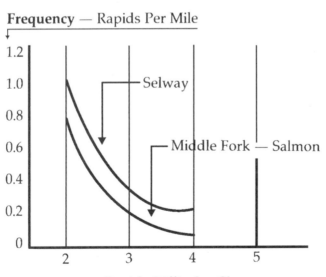

Frequency — Rapids Per Mile

Selway

Middle Fork — Salmon

Rapids Difficulty Class

17

This information indicates that for a particular set of flow conditions and a specific river section, the Selway and Middle Fork of the Salmon Rivers have similar rapids difficulty. However, the frequency of rapids per mile on the Selway is greater. The other rivers could be compared similarly. While experienced boaters who have run these rivers could have intuitively arrived at the same conclusion, this gives a quantitative evaluation for someone who has never run the rivers before. Boaters often refer to a river section as being a particular class run. It is important to know the class and frequency of rapids and whether major rapids may easily be portaged, since these can change the skills required.

It can be concluded that the boater with skills capable of boating Class 4 whitewater can run all the river sections in this book at moderate flows, with the possible exception of two Class 5 rapids on the Snake which could be portaged fairly easily by kayakers and with difficulty by rafters.

Drinking Water

In the past it was a common sight to see boaters with long handled dippers casually drinking water directly from the Middle Fork and Selway Rivers or from clear sidestreams on the other rivers. For the past several years there have been numerous problems with that troublesome protozoa, *Lambia Giardia*, and other river pollutants. Anyone who has ever experienced a full-blown case of "giardia" will be a true believer in treating all drinking or cooking water and paying special attention to personal and camp sanitation. The boater's equivalent of "Montezuma's Revenge" has an incubation period of about 18 days so that the only good thing is that the boater probably won't experience it on the river trip where it was contracted.

Suffice it to say that all water on all of these tours should be treated. Boiling is the simplest solution or using one of the better water purification filters.

Car Shuttling

Vehicle shuttling is one trip planning consideration common to all boaters. Most boaters who do not have the time to perform their own shuttle prefer to hire people in the area who make a business of shuttling. Shuttle driving is inherently seasonal and can involve transients with no responsibility or liability.

It makes sense that before entrusting your vehicle to a shuttle service and paying them a handsome sum, some inquiry be made about their reliability. The vehicle should be parked in a supervised area during the boating trip and delivered within a few hours of the take-out, with the drivers preferably meeting boaters. Leaving a vehicle overnight in an unattended transfer area, launch or take-out point is inviting vandalism.

Usually the river managing agency will provide a list of shuttle services on request. The list changes constantly, and since these services are not under agency permit, there is no implied responsibility.

SHUTTLE MAP

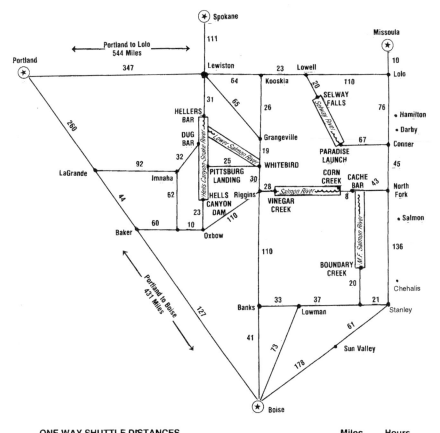

ONE WAY SHUTTLE DISTANCES		Miles	Hours
M.F. Salmon —	Boundary Creek to Cache Bar	220	6:00
Main Salmon —	Corn Creek to Vinegar Creek	408	9:30
Lower Salmon —	Whitebird to Hellers Bar	115	2:30
Selway —	Paradise Launch to Selway Falls	273	7:00
Hells Canyon of	Hells Canyon Dam to Dug Bar	127	4:30
the Snake —	Hells Canyon Dam to Pittsburg Landing	188	4:30
	Hells Canyon Dam to Hellers Bar	278	5:30

Wolf Creek Rapids — R.M. 127

THE SELWAY RIVER

In 1968 the Selway and the Middle Fork of the Salmon Rivers were included as two of only eight charter rivers in the National Wild and Scenic Rivers Act. Other Idaho rivers have since been included in the Wild and Scenic River System or are under study for inclusion. The instant designation of the Selway River in the Act suggests that this river has some obvious special qualities.

Originating in the Bitteroot Mountains, this westerly flowing river continues over 90 miles to Lowell, Idaho, where it meets its sister river, the Lochsa, merging with it to become the Clearwater River. In time the waters of the Selway combine with the Snake and the Columbia and ultimately flow into the Pacific Ocean. Bounded by the Bitteroot Mountains on the East, the Lochsa River on the North, the Salmon River on the South and rugged terrain to the West, the Selway Bitteroot Wilderness Area has resisted man's intrusion with partial success and maintained a wilderness quality. Centered within this wilderness area is the Selway River Tour, a roadless whitewater trip beginning at an elevation of 3,067 feet and ending 47 miles later at an elevation of 1,760 feet for an average river slope of 28 feet per mile.

The journey begins in a small, heavily forested canyon with frequent Class 1 and 2 rapids that become rock gardens at low flows and increase in difficulty at high river stages. Boaters agree that at high water some rapids increase one whole difficulty rating over moderate flows. The seven-mile section from Paradise Launch to Running Creek Ranch is relatively small but busy water with river slopes averaging 40 feet per mile. The boater will not see signs of civilization on this short section, as even the right bank trail is not visible, and most camps are small and inconspicuous. Shortly after the tour begins the canyon opens somewhat due to an old forest burn, but for the first seven miles to Running Creek Ranch the tour is in a small isolated river canyon.

Running Creek Ranch, at river mile 158, with its suspension bridge, airstrip and ranch is the first sign of civilization on the trip. This is one of six areas where boaters will see manmade improvements. The other areas are Shearer, North Star Ranch, Selway Lodge, Moose Creek and Three Links. Usually a trail suspension bridge or a rustic lodge is the extent of the visual impact. Boaters may wish to make a note of airstrips, ranches or forest service

Galloping Gertie Rapids — R.M. 159

Running Creek — R.M. 157

facilities at Moose Creek in case of an emergency. A trail roughly parallels the river the entire trip, although in some areas it does deviate from the river or climb high above it.

From Running Creek to Ham Rapids (R.M. 157-141) the river canyon widens, the river slope lessens and campsites in general are larger. Near Goat Creek the canyon again becomes forested with cedar, fir and pine forests which prevail throughout the remainder of the trip. Running Creek Camp is the first obvious, large, high water camp on the trip. For the most part rapids in this section are Class 2, and boaters begin to wonder about the Selway River stories they may have heard around the campfire. The one-third mile long Goat Creek Rapids provides a welcome whitewater challenge, and boaters cannot help but speculate how this rapids must appear at high water. One boater, describing Goat Creek Rapids at high water, commented: "If this is a Class 3 rapids, then Blossom Bar (Rogue River in Oregon) is a Class 1!" The short, Class 2 Rodeo Rapids is a play spot for kayakers to surf, do "endos" or practice catching the small eddy in a rock wall. The rapids are easy, the river is crystal clear and the scenery is spectacular — all of which tends to lead one to a complacency just before Ham Rapids.

Ham Rapids — R.M. 141

23

Ham Rapids is preceded by a short, Class 3 rapids. Ham itself is in a rocky narrow canyon, and is a difficult scout, which is probably why few people do scout Ham. The rapids is about two hundred yards long, with a large midstream boulder about halfway down. Virtually all of the water heads straight for this boulder, and it is difficult to decide which side to take. The left side is blind, the right is narrow but probably the best route. Ham is a steep drop, and large crafts develop an inertia hard to overcome, making maneuvering difficult. Skirting by the rock hazard on the right side in a kayak makes one consider Ham a Class 3 rapids, but those who hit the rock in a large raft, and possibly flip, tend to agree on the Class 4 rating. From Ham to Moose Creek is a series of about eight Class 2 rapids.

Moose Creek, which comes in at R.M. 138, is a major tributary of the Selway, adding about 50 percent to the flow. When reaching Moose Creek the boater recognizes he's in comparably larger water. The Selway and Moose Creek suspension bridges and trail system suggest that this is a good place to scout the next three-mile canyon section which contains the most difficult series of rapids on the trip. The pool and drop characteristic of this canyon section allow experienced boaters to scout from the river at low or moderate water levels, or to rely on reading the river as they boat, but first-time boaters often elect to scout from the trail. The Selway is not one of those rivers on which the boater simply aligns himself correctly at the top of the rapids and is assured of a favorable outcome. Some of the rapids are technical, requiring river reading and skillful maneuvering. For these reasons many first-time Selway boaters are willing to take the three-hour round trip to trail scout this canyon. Bring some good hiking boots, long pants, a camera and make this a planned part of the trip. The deterrents to trail hiking on the Selway are the snakes and occasional bear that may be seen. The trail system also allows boating passengers the option of walking around some rapids. While this usually isn't a necessary option at low water, it might be a good idea at high water. For most boaters this canyon is not a good place to be at high water.

Scouting is more of an attitude than a prerequisite for river running and depends on how the individual perceives river difficulty, skill, equipment and odds. The canyon section below Moose Creek is not the only section the boater may wish to scout. It is emphasized because of the frequency of major rapids within the short section. The advantage of trail scouting is that the boater is more likely to view the river from downstream, looking upstream

Double Drop Rapids — R.M. 137 *Al Ainsworth*

Wapoots Rapids — R.M. 137

Ladle Rapids Entrance — R.M. 136

Ladle Rapids — R.M. 136 *Al Ainsworth*

at the rapids. The holes that develop on the downstream side of boulders are more easily seen from this view. Often the boater fails to adequately scout the entire rapids from the river, as he is viewing rapids only from the upstream side. A slight boating error on the technical Selway River can change rapids difficulty significantly. First-time Selway boaters may wish to scout the following rapids: Galloping Gertie (R.M. 160), Ham (R.M. 141), the Canyon Section from Double Drop through Miranda Jane, Osprey (R.M. 132), Wolf Creek (R.M. 127) and Tee Kem Falls (R.M. 124). Scouting the main canyon allows greater opportunity for taking pictures, and it gives one a mental image of the three-mile slalom course. (Let's see now, it's right at Double Drop and left at Wapoots, avoiding the bottom hole, and right at Ladle, or was it left at Double Drop, and . . . ?) Scouting will also give the boater a great appreciation for the magnitude and the high water boating difficulty of the canyon. The logs on top of the natural dam at Little Niagara leave no doubt as to the location of high water, and the imagination is free to speculate on boating difficulty at that stage.

Tango Bar Rapids — R.M. 131

Wolf Creek Rapids — R.M. 127

Shortly after the rapids in the Main Canyon section, near river mile 133, the tempo of the river changes. There still are major rapids left, such as Osprey, Wolf Creek and Tee Kem Falls, but the river slope is changing. Pool sections become longer, rapids less frequent and the last seven miles are relatively flat water. This last section has some large cobble islands and a few sand beaches at low or moderate water levels deposited from flood stage.

Camps on the Selway vary a great deal, from marginal and scarce on the upper and canyon sections to large camps in some areas with sand beaches, convenient sidestreams, rapids for kayak play or holes for swimming or fishing. None of the camps have toilets. The Small, Medium or Large capacity rating indicates space for 8, 15 or 20 people. Since the maximum party size is 16, the medium and large camp sizes would generally accommodate the full party size. Some of the camps are unavailable at certain water stages, and Low, Moderate and High on the camp list refers to under 2.0, 2.0-4.0 and over 4.0 feet water levels on the Paradise gage. With only one launch per day allowed on the Selway, there should be no conflicts between parties, but some camp planning is necessary to allow for such things as trail scouting the main canyon. At high water boaters hurry through this trip, often in little more than two days. A more common trip length is four or more days.

Tee Kem Falls — R.M. 147 *Al Ainsworth*

Shuttling for the Selway trip is a major task. The two access routes to the Paradise Creek launch site are from Elk City, Idaho, on the west and from Conner, Montana, on the east. Ordinarily the Elk City route is not open until July. The majority of boaters shuttle via Conner, Montana, just south of Darby on route 93, by taking the West Fork Road (State Route 473) for 67 miles from Conner to the Paradise launch site. The one-way trip in to the launch takes about two hours and involves going over the 6,589 foot high Nez Perce Pass. Snow sometimes blocks the pass well into June. The one-way shuttle distance from Paradise Launch to Selway Falls take-out is 270 miles and takes seven hours of driving time.

Boaters have developed a rough scale of river difficulty for the Selway River similar to that on other Idaho rivers. Low difficulty is considered to be under 2.0 feet on the Paradise gage, moderate difficulty at 2.0-4.0 and high at anything over 4.0 feet. May and June are the predicted high water periods, leaving only a relatively short period for moderate or low water trips, from late June through mid-July, before the water is too low. Ordinarily boaters do not boat below 1.0 feet, and rafters prefer a 2.0 foot minimum. Boaters have boated the Selway between 0.6 and 8.0 Paradise gage height. However, these are generally considered the extreme limits. Flows at Paradise Launch are estimated to be about 25 percent of those at the Selway Falls take-out. Paradise gage data is available from the West Fork Ranger District.

The Selway, when boated at comparable water volumes, is more difficult than the other more popular Idaho tours such as The Middle Fork or Main Salmon Rivers. The problem in comparing the rivers is that most boaters do not boat the tours at comparable volumes. The Main Salmon, Lower Salmon and the Snake through Hells Canyon are inherently larger rivers, making comparison with the Selway difficult. As with most rivers, the degree of difficulty on the Selway increases markedly with river flow.

The Selway River is the least utilized permit river in the West. Over a 75-day permit season, from May 15 to August 1, one launch per day is allowed with a maximum party size of 16 people. Of the 1,200 people allowed to float the Selway during the permit season, only about 600 actually do so. In spite of the odds against getting a permit, the Selway is worth the effort, for it is one of the best white-water tours in the United States.

Selway Falls — R.M. 117   *Al Ainsworth*

Selway River Inventoried Campsites

River Mile	Name	Left or Right Bank	Camp Size Small, Medium, Large	Maximum Useable Water Level Low, Moderate, High
162.1	Bad Luck Bar	L	L	H
159.6	Waldo Bar	R	L	H
159.2	Driftwood Bar	L	M	M
159.0	Hungry Bear	L	S	L
157.6	Running Creek Bridge	L	L	M
157.4	Running Creek Flat	R	L	H
155.4	Archer	L	L	H
153.4	Goat Creek	L	S	H
152.4	Little Goat Creek	L	L	M
149.7	Cougar Flats	R	L	H
148.6	White Tail Flats	R	L	H
148.5	Mills	L	L	H
148.2	Bear Creek	R	S	L

River Mile	Name	Left or Right Bank	Camp Size Small, Medium, Large	Maximum Useable Water Level Low, Moderate, High
147.5	Unnamed	L	L	H
147.2	Big Cedar	R	M	L
146.4	Black Sands	L	L	M
145.6	Dead Elk	R	M	L
143.4	Rattlesnake Bar	R	M	H
140.3	Roots	L	S	M
138.3	Tony Point Bridge	R	M	H
138.2	Unnamed	L	M	M
138.1	Tony Point	L	M	H
137.4	Divide Creek	L	M	M
134.6	Upper Cedar Flats	R	S	L
134.2	Lower Cedar Flats	R	M	M
132.6	Meeker Creek	R	S	M
131.4	Tango Creek	R	M	H
131.3	Tango Bar	L	L	M
130.9	Trapper	L	M	L
128.3	Boulder Bar	R	M	M
128.0	Dry Bar	R	M	M
126.8	Upper Pinchot	R	M	M
126.6	Lower Pinchot	R	L	H
125.0	Ballinger	R	M	H
123.9	Tee Kem Falls	L	M	M
123.4	Cupboard Creek	R	M	M

Remainder of trip from Cupboard Creek to take-out near Meadow Creek has numerous camping beaches for medium and low water.

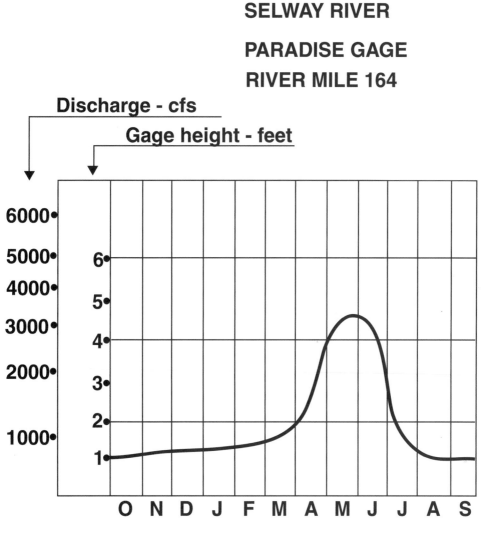

SELWAY RIVER

PARADISE GAGE
RIVER MILE 164

Discharge - cfs

Gage height - feet

Time - Months

Hazard - gage height
    Low - under 2
    Moderate - 2-4
    High - over 4

SELWAY RIVER LOG

River mile: 165 to 117 . . . . 47 miles

Drift time: 13 hours . . . . 4 m.p.h.

Logged in raft

River classification: Expert

River drop: 28 feet per mile average

River discharge: 1.7 feet, Paradise gage

Recommended discharge: 1.5-3.5 feet Paradise gage

River discharge information:

West Fork Ranger Station (Paradise gage)

(406) 821-3269

Information: permits, shuttle service, river flow

West Fork Ranger District

6735 West Fork Road

Darby, MT 59829

(406) 821-3269

Lottery permit applications December 1 through January 31.

Permit control season: May 15 through July 31.

LEGEND

MAP SYMBOLS

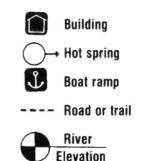

RM 95   River mile

Large camp

4   Rapids difficulty class

Bridge

Airstrip

Building

Hot spring

Boat ramp

Road or trail

River Elevation

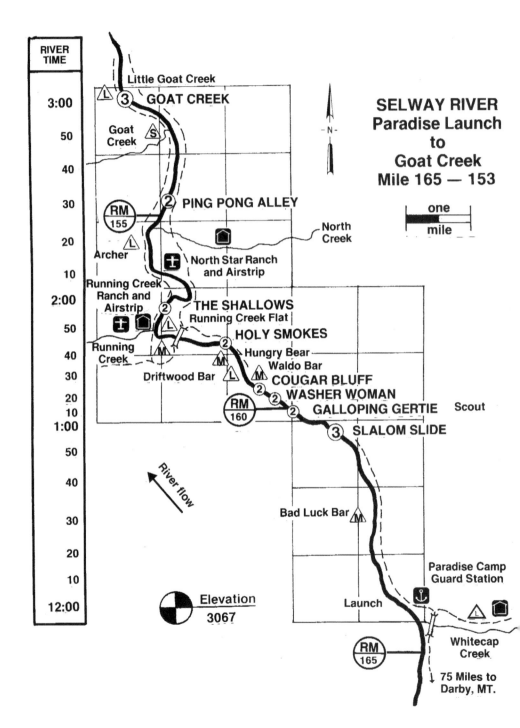

RIVER TIME

3:00
50
40
30
20
10
2:00
50
40
30
20
10
1:00
50
40
30
20
10
12:00

Little Goat Creek

GOAT CREEK

Goat Creek

PING PONG ALLEY

RM 155

North Creek

Archer

North Star Ranch and Airstrip

Running Creek Ranch and Airstrip

THE SHALLOWS
Running Creek Flat

HOLY SMOKES

Running Creek

Hungry Bear

Waldo Bar

Driftwood Bar

COUGAR BLUFF
WASHER WOMAN

RM 160

GALLOPING GERTIE   Scout

SLALOM SLIDE

River flow

Bad Luck Bar

Paradise Camp
Guard Station

Launch

Elevation
3067

Whitecap Creek

RM 165

↓ 75 Miles to Darby, MT.

SELWAY RIVER
Paradise Launch
to
Goat Creek
Mile 165 — 153

one
mile

-N-

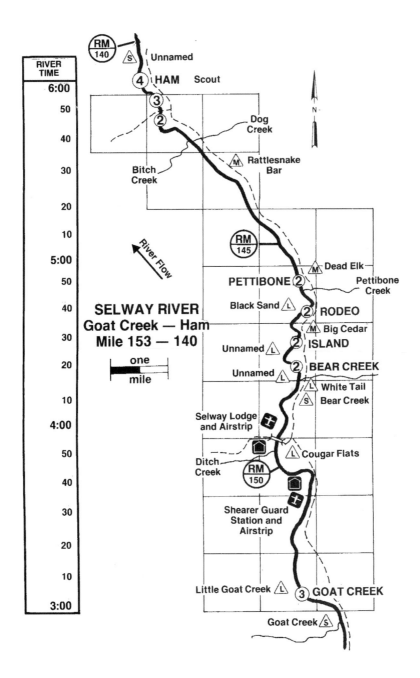

RIVER TIME

6:00
50
40
30
20
10
5:00
50
40
30
20
10
4:00
50
40
30
20
10
3:00

RM 140

Unnamed

4 HAM   Scout

3

2

Dog Creek

Rattlesnake Bar

Bitch Creek

River Flow

RM 145

Dead Elk

PETTIBONE 2

Pettibone Creek

SELWAY RIVER
Goat Creek — Ham
Mile 153 — 140

Black Sand

2 RODEO

Big Cedar

Unnamed

2 ISLAND

one
mile

Unnamed

2 BEAR CREEK

White Tail

Bear Creek

Selway Lodge and Airstrip

Cougar Flats

Ditch Creek

RM 150

Shearer Guard Station and Airstrip

Little Goat Creek

3 GOAT CREEK

Goat Creek

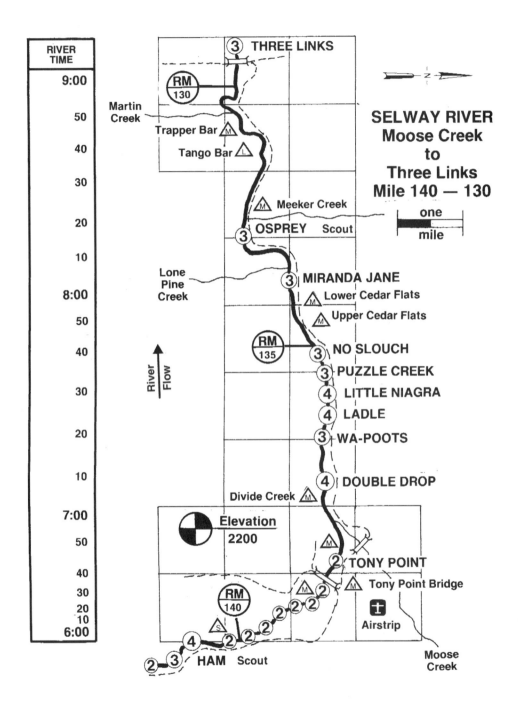

RIVER TIME

9:00
50
40
30
20
10
8:00
50
40
30
20
10
7:00
50
40
30
20
10
6:00

③ THREE LINKS

RM 130

Martin Creek

Trapper Bar M

Tango Bar L

M Meeker Creek

③ OSPREY Scout

Lone Pine Creek

③ MIRANDA JANE

M Lower Cedar Flats

M Upper Cedar Flats

RM 135

③ NO SLOUCH

③ PUZZLE CREEK

④ LITTLE NIAGRA

④ LADLE

③ WA-POOTS

④ DOUBLE DROP

Divide Creek M

River Flow

Elevation 2200

M

② TONY POINT

M Tony Point Bridge

RM 140

M ②

②②②

②

S

② ②

④

②③ HAM Scout

✝ Airstrip

Moose Creek

SELWAY RIVER
Moose Creek
to
Three Links
Mile 140 — 130

one
mile

38

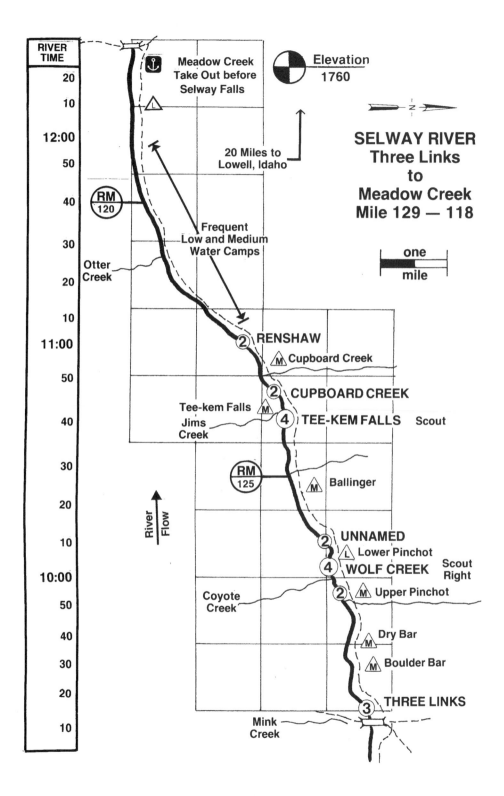

RIVER TIME

SELWAY RIVER
Three Links
to
Meadow Creek
Mile 129 — 118

Elevation
1760

Meadow Creek
Take Out before
Selway Falls

20 Miles to
Lowell, Idaho

one
mile

Frequent
Low and Medium
Water Camps

Otter
Creek

RM 120

RENSHAW ②
Cupboard Creek ⑩

CUPBOARD CREEK ②

Tee-kem Falls ⑩
TEE-KEM FALLS ④ Scout
Jims
Creek

RM 125
Ballinger ⑩

River
Flow

UNNAMED ②
Lower Pinchot ⑩
WOLF CREEK ④ Scout Right
Upper Pinchot ② ⑩

Coyote
Creek

Dry Bar ⑩

Boulder Bar ⑩

THREE LINKS ③

Mink
Creek

Elk Bar, Impassable Canyon — R.M. 17

Middle Fork of the Salmon River

The Middle Fork of the Salmon River starts in Central Idaho, northwesterly of Stanley, Idaho, in the shadow of 10,000-foot peaks of the Sawtooth Mountains. Capehorn and Marsh Creeks merge in an alpine setting to start the Middle Fork of the Salmon River. Early boat trips began near the origin of the Middle Fork, and later when a road was built to Dagger Falls, this was the common beginning of Middle Fork trips for years. The Dagger Falls boat launch has been removed and now trips begin one mile downstream at Boundary Creek Camp, where a new ramp and camp has been constructed at river mile 95.6. Trips terminate either at the confluence or, more usually, at the Cache Bar boat ramp about 3 miles downstream from the confluence on the Main Salmon. This gives whitewater boaters almost 100 miles of boating within the Idaho Primitive Area on a charter river in the National Wild and Scenic River System.

The Middle Fork tour starts near an elevation of 5,700 feet dropping almost 2,700 feet, to an elevation of 3,015 at the river's confluence with the Main Salmon, for an average loss in elevation of 28 feet per mile.

The elevation change, in addition to the change in river flow, divides the trip into three sections. The upper section from Boundary Creek to Pistol Creek (22 miles), the central section from Pistol Creek to Big Creek (56 miles) and the Lower Canyon section from Big Creek to the confluence with the Main Salmon (18 miles).

The upper section from Boundary Creek to Pistol Creek is characterized by a heavily wooded, steep and relatively narrow canyon. The river flow is noticeably small by comparison to the lower sections and is probably less than half of the Middle Fork Lodge flows. There are few eddies, and consequently, stopping can be difficult at high river discharges. The upper section drops from an elevation of about 5,700 feet to 4,735 for an average drop of 42 feet per mile.

Immediately on leaving the Boundary Creek launch, you come into whitewater that goes at least to Velvet Falls. The combination of river velocity and rocky channel present a condition of unstable channel flow where miniature "haystacks" form the continuous sections of whitewater. The river seems to dance from this release of energy, requiring the boater's full attention in this upper section.

The rapids are almost continuous Class 1 and 2 blending occasionally into Class 3 rapids. At high flows Velvet Falls, Powerhouse and Pistol Creek are Class 4 rapids. Although boatmen experienced with the Middle Fork seldom scout any rapids, the majority of boaters floating the Middle Fork for the first time scout Sulphur Slide, Velvet Falls and Pistol Creek rapids. There are other rapids equally as difficult as Sulphur Slide, however, their difficulty in scouting makes river reading a reasonable alternative. Ramshorn Narrows, Second Narrows, The Chutes, Elkhorn, Powerhouse, Artillery or Cannon rapids are exciting, yet more frequently than not, they are seldom scouted.

The upper section is definitely not a pool and drop river. The few pools or large eddies such as Gardells Hole or Dolly Lake are conspicuous in this section. Many of the river camps are small and correspond more to refuge camps, easily missed as the busy boater concentrates on rapids rather than camp watching. The eddies and sandy beaches so desirable for camps seldom exist in this section, particularly at high water. These same conditions make scouting Velvet Falls difficult. The large rock on the left that is the landmark for "Velvet," is just one in a canyon full of rocks. By the time you do identify this rock, it may already be too late to scout, or at high water, impossible to pull behind the rock to run the falls on the left. At low flows "Velvet" is much easier to deal with.

Velvet Falls — R.M. 90

When river flows are less than 1,500 c.f.s. at the Middle Fork Lodge gage, this upper section becomes marginally unrunnable because of low water, and many boaters either fly into the Indian Creek airstrip to avoid low flows or to shorten the trip. Actually, the upper section is one of the most exciting whitewater sections of the entire trip, so try not to miss this part of the tour. Perhaps the most common mistake on the Middle Fork is boating at too high a discharge. The more notable accidents on the Middle Fork have occurred at high flows. For an account of one high water trip, read *The Big Drops* by Collins and Nash.

Dolly Lake — R.M. 76

Pistol Creek Rapids — R.M. 74

Sunflower Flat Hotsprings — R.M. 62

By the time you pass Pistol Creek, you are below the sub-alpine, densely forested small canyon area. The canyon broadens, trees are mostly Ponderosa Pine, rapids are no longer continuous and the river slope is changing to an average drop of 23 feet per mile. Temperatures should be warmer, and you exchange mosquitoes or "no-seeums" for poison ivy and the potential for rattlesnakes. Airstrips and cabins remind the boater that true wilderness may be hard to find. To compensate, the camps are larger and generally very desirable. Five of the seven hot spring camps are in this section. Bathing in the hot springs makes some camps a memorable part of the trip, even with the poison ivy we found at Whitie Cox Camp hot spring, or the rattlesnake guarding the hot spring near Hood Ranch.

Campsites are assigned with the trip permit at time of launch. Boaters are limited to one camp per trip below Big Creek (R.M. 18) and party size dictates camp assignments. Camp areas such as Indian Creek airstrip (R.M. 68) are restricted along with other cultural resource protected camps. There is high competition for some camps, and boaters are limited to one hot springs camp per trip. There are some camps, particularly in the upper section, that are low water camps. Fortunately most camps are adequate at high water. Camp planning is obviously a necessity for a Middle Fork trip.

The rapids in this central section from Pistol Creek to Big Creek are for the most part very ordinary with probably no more than a dozen Class 3 rapids in this 56-mile section. The boater may only scout Tappen Falls and Haystack Rapids.

You should take some time to hike or explore historical sites. Part of this central section is within the "Impassable Canyon." The Impassable Canyon starts near Bernard Airstrip and Haystack Rapids at river mile 27. With luck you may spot some of the sheep that range in the 4,000-foot canyon walls starting, at least, near Hospital Bar Hot Springs and continuing to the trip end. The canyon walls on the left bank near Tappan Ranch are nothing short of spectacular. The book, *Middle Fork and the Sheepeater War*, gives many historical spots where the boater could select side trips, depending on his time and inclination for exploring. There are trails on one, or sometimes, both sides of the river in this section. The ranches, old cabins and mining relics serve as a reminder of Middle Fork early history. The several airstrips serve as communicative links for both ranches and boaters flying in fresh food for this five-day plus trip. Seven of the eight airstrips on the total trip are in this central section. In the case of an emergency, the airstrips are a tolerable intrusion on the wilderness, and during low water, people are often flown into Indian Creek to begin their trip.

The canyon is changing constantly throughout this central 56-mile section. It is, however, different enough from the upper sub-alpine section or the lower part of the "Impassable Canyon" section to make this a distinct and different part of the river trip. In this central section you will drop about 1,340 feet in elevation, for an average of 23 feet per mile, and varying from an elevation of 4,700 to 3,400 feet.

One unique feature of the Middle Fork trip is the last 18-mile section of the "Impassable Canyon" from the Big Creek to the confluence with the Main Salmon River.

This canyon starts dramatically just beyond Big Creek where vertical rock walls are the beginning of a narrow canyon that continues to the river mouth. There are no continuous trails, airstrips or people living beyond Big Creek. By now the river has doubled in volume over the Middle Fork Lodge flows. The rapids are very different from those encountered at the trip beginning. Camps are fewer in this section, and those that exist are sometimes small and rocky. Wind becomes more noticeable, complicating boating and camping. You will see huge caves and small waterfalls spilling over

Middle Fork Lodge — R.M. 61

47

Kayak Play Spot — R.M. 52

Whitie Cox Grave — R.M. 49

Whitie Cox Hot Springs — R.M. 49

Loon Creek Cabin — R.M. 46

Hospital Bar Hot Springs — R.M. 43

Sheep near Hospital Bar — R.M. 42

Grouse Creek Cabin — R.M. 39

Tappan Falls — R.M. 37

Tappan Island — R.M. 38

Haystack Rapids — R.M. 28

the canyon rims as the falls dissolve in spray before hitting the bottom. Indian rock paintings can be observed in several of the caves. Rapids that you may scout in this section are Redsides, Weber and Rubber. It would be easy to miss locating these rapids and be forced into running them blind unless the boater pays attention to the log. The most exciting part of this section of big water rapids is from Cliffside to the confluence. It contains half a dozen Class 3 rapids in addition to Rubber Rapids, which can be one of the most difficult on the river. This section will end your Middle Fork trip in a memorable way.

The Middle Fork provides a wide range of whitewater experiences, ranging from low volume water and steep river slopes to the big water in the lower canyon. In between, there are miles of relatively easy river. The strong Class 3 boater, willing to scout and use caution, should find this an enjoyable trip, unless the mistake is made of boating at high water (and risk). The keys to a safe trip on the Middle Fork are the river volume and being prepared for the wide range in environment which may change from snow and thunderstorms to high temperatures.

Many boaters prefer to run at optimum flows of 1,500-3,000 c.f.s. Somewhere near 4,000 c.f.s. most boaters agree that the river

Diving Rock, near Woolard Creek — R.M. 21

Stoddard Creek Pictographs — R.M. 6

becomes hazardous and a few have added another bench mark by terming flows over 6,500 c.f.s. as suicidal. The upper section becomes unrunnable at discharges less than about 800 c.f.s., or a gage reading of about 2.2. All flows are referenced to the Middle Fork Lodge gage. Optimum, suicidal, low, high or moderate are adjectives dependent primarily on equipment, skills and attitudes of the individual. Most boaters generally agree to the approximate following table of gage height, discharge and hazard rating.

Hazard Rating	Gage Height-Feet	Discharge-c.f.s.
Low	2.5-3.5	1000-2500
Moderate	3.5-5.0	2500-4400
High	over 5.0	over 4400

Whatever river discharge you prefer, the Middle Fork of the Salmon provides one of the better whitewater experiences in America.

Middle Fork of the Salmon River Camps

River Mile	Name	Left or Right Bank	Camp Size Small, Medium, Large	Comment
95.6	Boundary Creek Launch	L	L	
95	Tepee Hole	L	S	Low water
94	Cable Hole	L	S	Low water
93	Gardells Hole	R	M	Low water
92	Cold Spring	L	S	Low water
90	Ramshorn	L	S	
90	Velvet Falls	L	S	Low water
89	Boy Scout	R	M	Low water
88	Big Bend	R	L	Low water
88	Trail Flat	L	L	Hot spring
87	Rapid	L	S	
87	Elkhorn Bar	R	L	
85	Saddle	L	M	Low water
85	Boot	R	S	
83	Joe Bump Cabin	L	L	
82	Scout	L	M	Hot spring
82	Sheepeater	L	L	Hot spring
81	Fire Island	L	L	
80	Lake Creek	R	M	
80	Johns	R	L	
80	Oakie Point	L	M	
79	Greyhound Creek	R	M	Low water
79	Dome Hole	L	M	Low water
77	Rapid River	R	L	
76	Big Snag	L	L	
76	Dolly Lake	R	L	Low water
74	Quick Stop	R	S	
74	Pistol Creek	L	L	
73	Airplane	L	L	
70	Indian Creek Landing Field	L	L	Restricted
70	Packbridge	L	M	Low water
68	Upper Indian Creek (airstrip)	L	L	Restricted
68	Lower Indian Creek	L	L	
67	Pungo Creek	L	L	Restricted
64	Little Soldier	R	L	Low water

River Mile	Name	Left or Right Bank	Camp Size Small, Medium, Large	Comment
63	Upper Marble Creek	L	L	
63	Lower Marble Creek #2	R	M	
62	Lost Oak	L	L	
62	Sunflower Flat	R	S	Hot springs
60	State Land	L	L	
59	Little Creek	R	L	Low water
59	Hood Ranch	L	L	Hot springs
57	Upper Jackass	R	L	
57	Lower Jackass Flat	R	L	Restricted
55	Cameron Creek	L	M	
53	Mahoney	R	S	Low water
51	Pine Creek Flat	R	L	
49	Culver Creek	R	S	
48	Whitie Cox	R	L	Hot springs
48	Rock Island	L	L	Restricted
48	Pebble Beach	L	L	
47	White Creek	R	M	Restricted
46	Shelf	R	S	
45	Big Loon	R	L	Hot springs
45	Cow Creek	L	S	Restricted
43	Cave	R	S	
43	Hospital Bar	L	L	Hot springs
43	Horsetail	R	S	
42	Cub Creek	L	S	
39	Upper Grouse Creek	R	L	
39	Lower Grouse Creek	R	L	
38	Tappan Island	Island	M	
35	Camas Creek	R	L	
35	Johnny Walker	L	L	
34	Pool	R	S	
34	Funston	L	M	
33	Broken Oar	R	S	
32	Normandy	L	S	
32	Trail	R	L	Low water
31	Sheep Creek	L	L	
29	Flying "B"	R	S	
28	Flying "B" Airport	R	L	
27	Bernard	L	L	
27	Short Creek	R	S	
26	Cold Spring	R	S	

River Mile	Name	Left or Right Bank	Camp Size Small, Medium, Large	Comment
25	Little Pine	L	L	
24	Driftwood Flat	R	L	
23	Wilson Creek	R	L	
23	#1 Upper Grassy Flat	L	L	
23	#2 Lower Grassy Flat	L	L	
21	Survey Creek	L	L	
21	Woolard Creek	R	L	
20	Fly	R	S	Low water
19	Fish	L	S	Low water
18	Big Creek	L	S	
18	Last Chance	R	M	
18	Pine Bluff	L	M	Low water
18	Cutthroat Cove	L	S	
17	Big Pine	R	S	
17	Elk Bar	L	L	Low water
17	Love Bär	L	M	Low water
14	Redside	L	S	
12	Papoose	L	S	Low water
12	Ship Island	L	L	
11	Lightning Strike	L	S	Low water
10	Parrot Placer	R	L	Low water
8	Parrott Cabin	L	M	
7	Cradle Creek	R	M	Low water
7	Tumble Creek	R	L	
6	Ouzel	L	S	
6	Cliffside	R	L	Low water
6	Stoddard	L	L	
6	Otter Bar	R	L	Low water
4	Solitude	L	S	Low water
1	Goat Creek	R	S	

Camps listed as low water may be inundated, or the camp area reduced, at moderate or high flows. Restricted camps may be closed for cultural resource protection. One night camp limitation per trip below Big Creek (R.M. 18).

MIDDLE FORK
SALMON RIVER
MIDDLE FORK LODGE GAGE
RIVER MILE 61

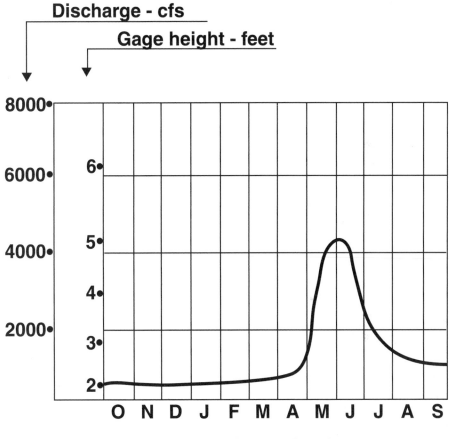

Time - Months

Hazard

> Low - 2.5-3.5 feet
> Moderate - 3.5-5 feet
> High - over 5 feet

MIDDLE FORK OF THE SALMON RIVER LOG

River mile: 96.5 to mouth . . . . 97 miles

Drift time: 21 hours . . . . 4.6 m.p.h.

Logged in raft

River classification: Expert

River drop: 28 feet per mile average

River discharge: 1,300-2,100 c.f.s.

Recommended discharge: 1,500-3,000 c.f.s.

Middle Fork Lodge gage

River discharge information:

Boise National Weather Service

(208) 334-9860

Information: permits, shuttle service, river flow

Middle Fork Ranger District

Highway 93N

P.O. Box 750

Challis, Idaho 83226

(208) 879-4101

Lottery permit applications December 1 through January 31.

Permits required all year.

Lottery permit season May 28 through September 3.

LEGEND

MAP SYMBOLS

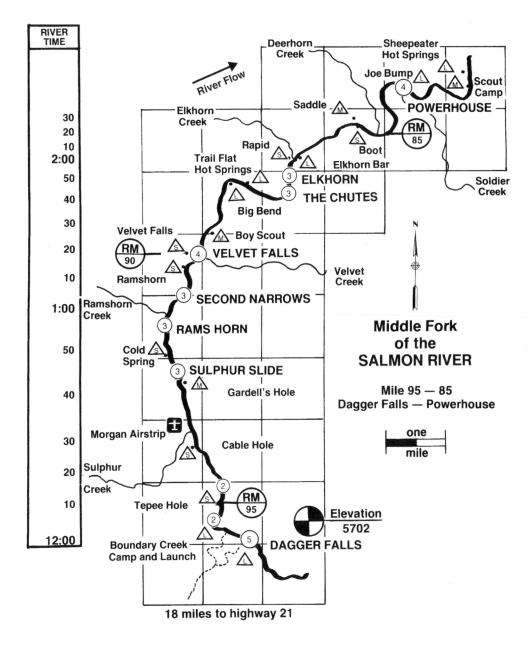

RIVER TIME

- 30
- 20
- 10
- **2:00**
- 50
- 40
- 30
- 20
- 10
- **1:00**
- 50
- 40
- 30
- 20
- 10
- **12:00**

River Flow

Deerhorn Creek

Sheepeater Hot Springs

Joe Bump

Scout Camp

POWERHOUSE

Saddle

RM 85

Soldier Creek

Elkhorn Creek

Rapid

Boot

Elkhorn Bar

Trail Flat Hot Springs

ELKHORN

THE CHUTES

Big Bend

Boy Scout

Velvet Falls

RM 90

VELVET FALLS

Velvet Creek

Ramshorn

Ramshorn Creek

SECOND NARROWS

RAMS HORN

Cold Spring

SULPHUR SLIDE

Gardell's Hole

Morgan Airstrip

Cable Hole

Sulphur Creek

Tepee Hole

RM 95

Elevation 5702

Boundary Creek Camp and Launch

DAGGER FALLS

18 miles to highway 21

N

Middle Fork
of the
SALMON RIVER

Mile 95 — 85
Dagger Falls — Powerhouse

one
mile

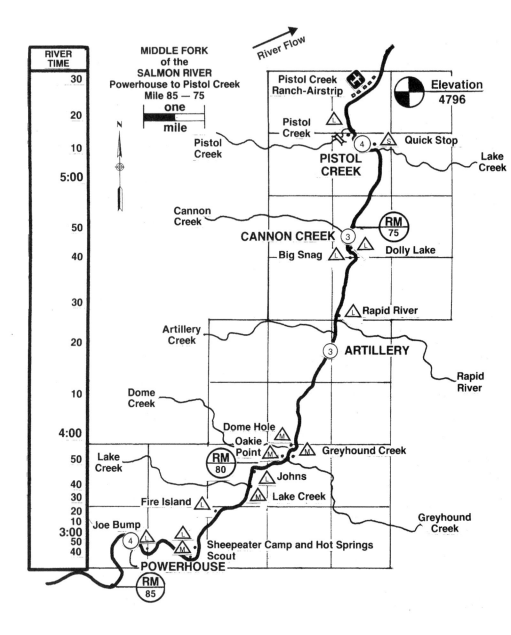

MIDDLE FORK
of the
SALMON RIVER
Powerhouse to Pistol Creek
Mile 85 — 75

one
mile

N

River Flow

Pistol Creek
Ranch-Airstrip

Elevation
4796

Pistol
Creek

Pistol
Creek

Quick Stop

**PISTOL
CREEK**

Lake
Creek

Cannon
Creek

CANNON CREEK

RM
75

Big Snag

Dolly Lake

Rapid River

Artillery
Creek

ARTILLERY

Dome
Creek

Rapid
River

Dome Hole

Oakie
Point

Greyhound Creek

RM
80

Lake
Creek

Johns

Fire Island

Lake Creek

Greyhound
Creek

Joe Bump

Sheepeater Camp and Hot Springs
Scout

POWERHOUSE

RM
85

RIVER
TIME

30
20
10
5:00

50
40

30

20

10
4:00

50

40
30
20
10
3:00
50
40

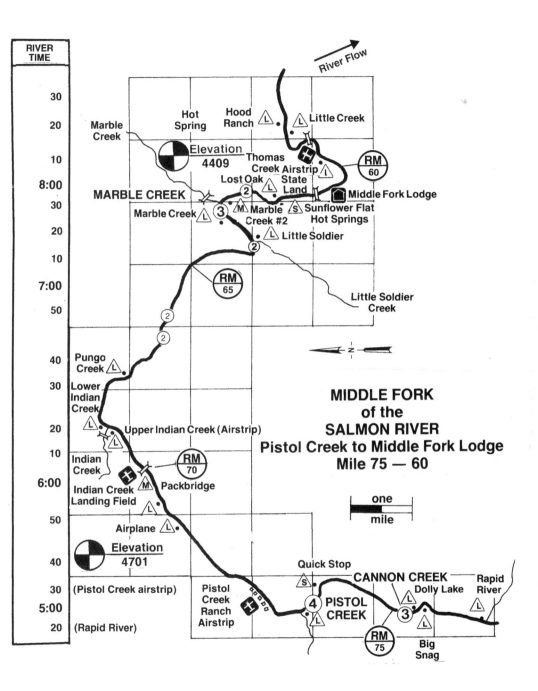

MIDDLE FORK
of the
SALMON RIVER
Pistol Creek to Middle Fork Lodge
Mile 75 — 60

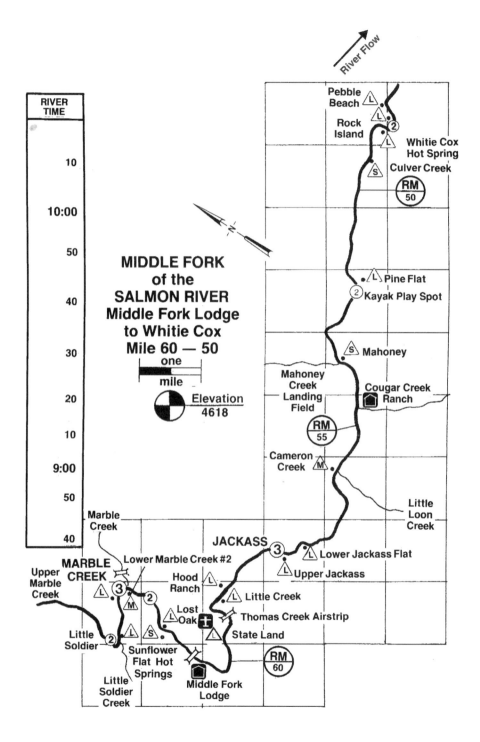

River Flow

RIVER TIME

10

10:00

50

40

30

20

10

9:00

50

40

MIDDLE FORK
of the
SALMON RIVER
Middle Fork Lodge
to Whitie Cox
Mile 60 — 50

one
mile

Elevation
4618

Pebble Beach

Rock Island

Whitie Cox Hot Spring

Culver Creek

RM 50

Pine Flat

Kayak Play Spot

Mahoney

Mahoney Creek Landing Field

Cougar Creek Ranch

RM 55

Cameron Creek

Little Loon Creek

Marble Creek

JACKASS

Lower Marble Creek #2

Lower Jackass Flat

MARBLE CREEK

Upper Jackass

Upper Marble Creek

Hood Ranch

Little Creek

Lost Oak

Thomas Creek Airstrip

Little Soldier

State Land

Sunflower Flat Hot Springs

Little Soldier Creek

Middle Fork Lodge

RM 60

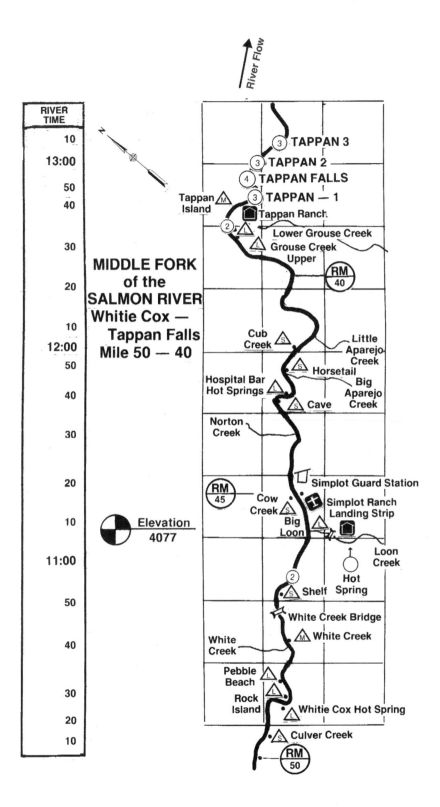

River Flow

RIVER TIME

10
13:00
50
40
30
20
10
12:00
50
40
30
20
10
11:00
50
40
30
20
10

MIDDLE FORK
of the
SALMON RIVER
Whitie Cox —
Tappan Falls
Mile 50 — 40

Elevation
4077

③ TAPPAN 3
③ TAPPAN 2
④ TAPPAN FALLS
③ TAPPAN — 1
Tappan Island Ⓜ
Tappan Ranch
② Ⓛ Lower Grouse Creek
Ⓛ Grouse Creek Upper
RM 40

Cub Creek Ⓢ
Little Aparejo Creek
Ⓢ Horsetail
Big Aparejo Creek
Hospital Bar Hot Springs Ⓛ
Ⓢ Cave
Norton Creek

Simplot Guard Station
RM 45
Cow Creek Ⓢ
Simplot Ranch Landing Strip
Big Loon Ⓛ
Loon Creek
Hot Spring
②
Ⓢ Shelf
White Creek Bridge
Ⓜ White Creek
White Creek
Pebble Beach Ⓛ
Rock Island Ⓛ
Ⓛ Whitie Cox Hot Spring
Ⓢ Culver Creek
RM 50

67

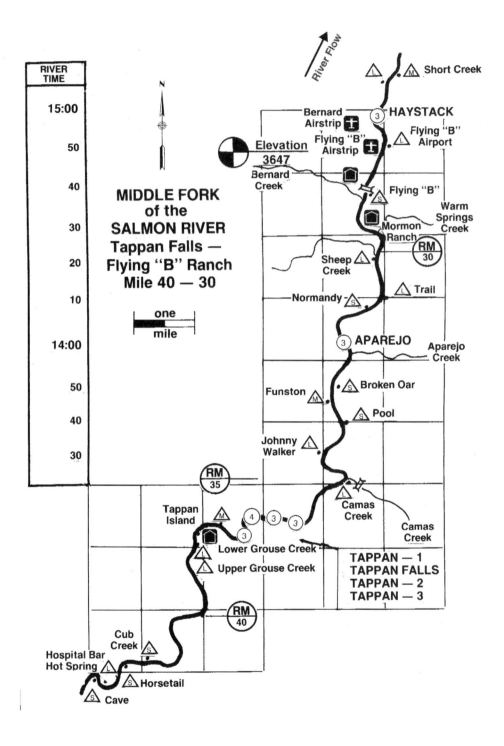

MIDDLE FORK
of the
SALMON RIVER
Tappan Falls —
Flying "B" Ranch
Mile 40 — 30

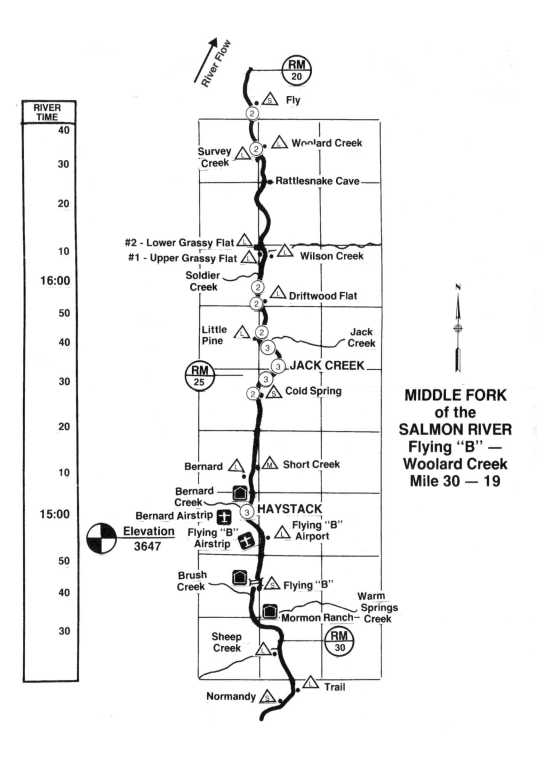

RM 20

S Fly
2

2 Woolard Creek
Survey Creek

Rattlesnake Cave

#2 - Lower Grassy Flat
#1 - Upper Grassy Flat   Wilson Creek
Soldier Creek
2
2 Driftwood Flat
2
Little Pine   2   Jack Creek
3
3 JACK CREEK
RM 25   3
2 S Cold Spring

Bernard   M Short Creek
Bernard Creek
Bernard Airstrip   3 HAYSTACK
Elevation 3647   Flying "B" Airstrip   Flying "B" Airport
Brush Creek   S Flying "B"
Warm Springs Creek
Mormon Ranch
Sheep Creek   RM 30
Normandy S   Trail

RIVER TIME
40
30
20
10
16:00
50
40
30
20
10
15:00
50
40
30

N

MIDDLE FORK of the SALMON RIVER Flying "B" — Woolard Creek Mile 30 — 19

69

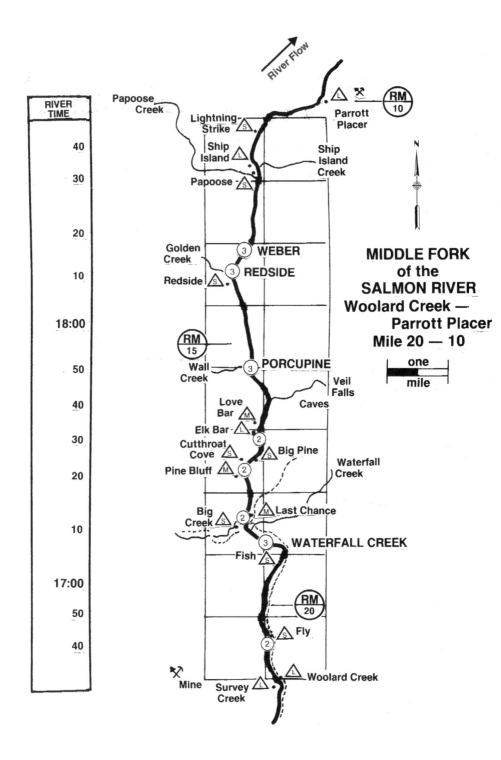

River Flow

RIVER TIME

40
30
20
10
18:00
50
40
30
20
10
17:00
50
40

Papoose Creek
Lightning-Strike
Ship Island
Papoose

Parrott Placer

RM 10

Ship Island Creek

N

Golden Creek
Redside

3 WEBER
3 REDSIDE

MIDDLE FORK
of the
SALMON RIVER
Woolard Creek —
Parrott Placer
Mile 20 — 10

RM 15

Wall Creek
3 PORCUPINE

Veil Falls

Love Bar
Elk Bar
Cutthroat Cove
Pine Bluff

Caves

2
S Big Pine
2

Waterfall Creek

one
mile

Big Creek
S 2
M Last Chance
3 WATERFALL CREEK

Fish S

RM 20

2 S Fly

Mine
Survey Creek
L Woolard Creek

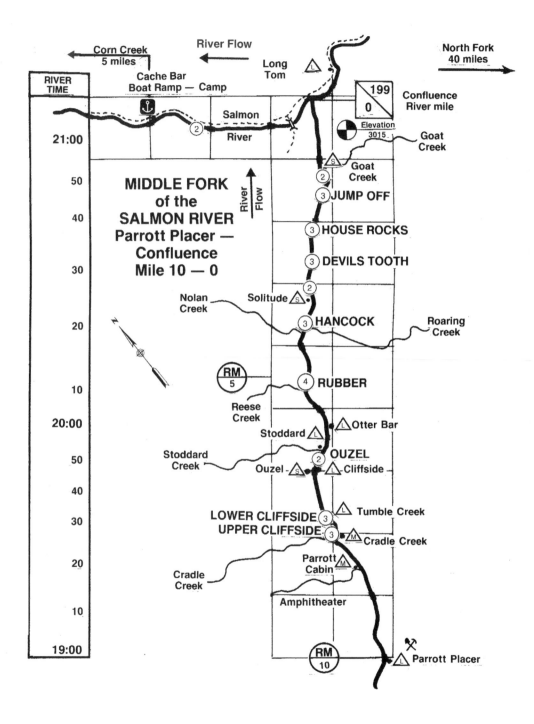

MIDDLE FORK
of the
SALMON RIVER
Parrott Placer —
Confluence
Mile 10 — 0

River Flow

Corn Creek
5 miles

North Fork
40 miles

Long
Tom

Cache Bar
Boat Ramp — Camp

Salmon

River

Confluence
River mile

199
0

Elevation
3015

Goat
Creek

Goat
Creek

JUMP OFF

HOUSE ROCKS

DEVILS TOOTH

Nolan
Creek

Solitude

HANCOCK

Roaring
Creek

RM
5

RUBBER

Reese
Creek

Otter Bar

Stoddard

OUZEL

Stoddard
Creek

Ouzel

Cliffside

Tumble Creek

LOWER CLIFFSIDE
UPPER CLIFFSIDE

Cradle Creek

Parrott
Cabin

Cradle
Creek

Amphitheater

RM
10

Parrott Placer

RIVER
TIME

21:00

50

40

30

20

10

20:00

50

40

30

20

10

19:00

Buckskin Bill — (Sylvan A. Hart)

The Main Salmon

"River of No Return"

The most popular overnight wilderness section of the 425-mile Salmon River is a 79-mile trip from Corn Creek to Vinegar Creek. This is a roads-end to roads-end section starting approximately at the Mouth of the Middle Fork of the Salmon and ending 28 miles upstream from Riggins, Idaho. The "River of No Return" is considered longer than this section. However, the roadless section between Corn Creek and Vinegar Creek make this section more remote and desirable than other sections of the river. The 425-mile Salmon River begins at elevations above 8,000 feet in the Sawtooth mountains and ends at its confluence with the Snake River at an elevation of 905 feet and drains 14,000 square miles. Next to Hells Canyon of the Snake River this is the deepest gorge on the continent. The Middle Fork of the Salmon is a popular trip often combined with the Main Salmon. Both rivers require reservation type permits. The Lower Salmon, which presently requires no permit, or Hells Canyon of the Snake River or the Selway are other possible alternates for the river runner to consider with the Main Salmon trip.

The Lewis and Clark expedition decided this river section was probably impassable by boat, or foot, and the legendary "River of No Return" carries many ominous concerns to most boaters. This section of the Salmon River, during the time of year the expedition would have boated it, is far less hazardous than many other rivers these capable explorers did boat enroute to the Pacific Ocean. Actually, jet boats ply this section regularly in both directions at reasonable river stages. Downriver floaters alone account for more than 8,000 people per season, and except for two Class 4 rapids (Salmon Falls and Big Mallard), this is essentially a big water Class 3 river considered less difficult than the Middle Fork when boated at comparable river discharges.

River hazard can be related to discharge, and the Corn Creek gage has a hazard rating where below 5,000 c.f.s. is low, 5,000-10,000 medium, over 10,000 high. This is not a regular U.S. Geological Survey gage, and gage heights or discharge can be obtained from the Forest Service at North Fork, Idaho. The river trip has an average gradient of 12 feet per mile, and the rapids are almost all of the pool and drop type.

The trip starts in a relatively large canyon with few trees, then quickly changes to a V-shape with large predominantly pine evergreen forests. The high water mark is easily recognizable by a distinct tree line and change in vegetation. Few large eddies exist at high water, and the 12 feet per mile average trip slope is deceptive. What sand beaches do exist on this trip are deposited at high water, making many camps essentially low water camps that would be flooded out at high river discharge. It isn't until you are almost to Big Mallard rapids, near river mile 154, that you begin to see high benches or terraces that could provide high water camp refuges. Many of the camps have boulder beaches at most all stages. Careful camp planning becomes important because of the competition for those that exist. Camps are not assigned on the Main Salmon.

What is surprising on this trip are the large stands of predominantly pine timber during almost the entire trip. This is in sharp contrast to the area near Riggins, Idaho, and the Lower Salmon, which is almost completely devoid of trees. The trip starts near an elevation of 2,929 feet, creating cool days even in August until near the end of the trip. We saw a few sheep, deer, otters, ducks, eagles and a beaver. However, August is probably not the best time to see

Salmon Falls — R.M. 170

the deer and elk that are supposed to be so plentiful, particularly in the "Salmon River Breaks" area.

The Salmon River has many cabins or old mine sites that could be explored along the way. The book, *River of No Return*, offers many sources for side trips, and outlines the early history of this area. Some of the old accounts of river running, when Salmon River boating was considered almost a death defying act, make interesting reading. Today all manner of craft use the Salmon, some in plastic boats hardly larger than a child's bathtub. Obviously, the Salmon is not child's play at high water when rapids such as Salmon Falls, Big Mallard, Elkhorn or Chittam should concern anyone.

The major rapids on this section occur between Corn Creek and Mackay Bar (56 miles). From Mackay Bar to the Vinegar Creek take-out is about 22 miles of flat water with only Dried Meat and Chittam rapids that are of concern. Some boaters, who can alter their concept of the "wilderness," end their trip at Mackay Bar Resort. From there you can be shuttled back upstream in a few hours by jetboat to the Corn Creek Camp origin of your trip. The increasing cost of shuttles makes this an economically competitive

Big Mallard Rapids — R.M. 154

Greg Smith

Buckskin Bill's Fort — R.M. 138

means of shuttling for those who wish to avoid the last flat water section or who want to depart from Corn Creek rather than the Riggins, Idaho, area.

In former years an interesting side trip was the stop at "Buckskin Bill's" cabin. This famous hermit actually loved to socialize with people and would share stories of his forty-five years on the Salmon. Although Bill has been dead now for some years, his buildings and the legend remain as part of the Salmon River lore. Anyone who has the good fortune to be near The Idaho Primitive Area should attempt to take this trip which, in spite of its jet boats, is one of the most primitive areas remaining in the contiguous 48 states.

There are just over 100 inventoried camps on the Main Salmon, or an average of over one per mile. They are fairly evenly distributed with the maximum distance between camps approximately three miles. Camp capacity is rated as small for camp size of less than 10 persons, medium for 10-20 and large for 30 persons. Although some of the large camps could have a capacity of over 30 persons, this is the maximum allowable party size. The majority of inventoried camps is large. There are no toilets at camps, meaning that the carry-out policy for human waste is a necessary part of trip planning.

Regulations change as plans are being implemented, so the boater should inquire before any trip to make certain of recent regulations and that the party can meet launch requirements. Boaters can expect open fire restrictions during the summer season.

Trails parallel the river on the right or north bank throughout most of the trip, excepting from Lantz Bar to Dillinger Creek (mile 180-162) and from Mackay Bar resort to Polly Bemis ranch (mile 134-124) and Sheep Creek to Chittam Creek (116-113). There is an airstrip at Mackay Bar resort.

Main Salmon River Camps

River Mile	Name	Left or Right Bank	Camp Size Small, Medium, Large	Comment
190.5	Corn Creek - camp, launch	R	L	
187.5	Lunch Bars			3 low water beaches
186.9	Horse Creek - upper	R	L	
186.8	Horse Creek - lower	R	M	
186.4	Stub Creek - upper	L	S	Low water - outfitter's camp
185.7	Legend Creek	R	M	High water
184.2	Spindle Creek	R	L	Low water
183.5	Cottonwood Creek (Bar)	R	L	Fast water
182.5	Phantom Creek	R	M	Moderate water high beach, low water beach
181.6	Alder Creek	L	L	Low water
180.5	Otter Creek	L	S	Low water
180.3	Fawn Creek	R	M	High water
179.8	Lantz Bar - upper	R	M	Sloping beach
180.0	Lantz Bar - cabins	R	L	High bench
179.9	Little Squaw Creek (Lantz)	R	L	Rocky bar
179.4	Tag Creek	L	M	High water - high bank
178.9	Disappointment Creek	L	L	High water - high bank
177.5	Devils Teeth - upper	R	M	Low water
177.4	Devils Toe Creek	L	L	High water - rocky bank
175.5	Elkhorn Creek	R	L	High water - rocky bank
175.2	Chamberlain Creek	L	S	Rocky site
174.5	Chukar Beach	R	M	Low water
173.9	Blackadar Hole	R	L	High water bench
173.4	Motor	L	L	Low water
172.7	Big Squaw Creek - lower	R	M	Low water
171.6	Smith Gulch-outfitters camp	R	L	Rocky bank
170.9	Corey Bar - upper	R	L	Fast water
167.8	Sunny Bar	R	L	Rocky bar before Island Opposite Hot Spring High rocky bank
167.7	Barth Hot Springs	L	L	High above Hot Spring
167.5	Barth Hot Springs - lower	L	L	Rocky bank
166.7	Sandy Hole	R	M	Low water
166.4	Nixon Bar	L	L	High water - rocky
166.4	Poor Bar (at Nixon Creek)	L	L	High rocky bank
165.4	Bruin Creek	L	M	Fast water - rocky landing
164.8	Bear Creek	R	L	Rocky bank
163.7	Sandy Beach	L	M	Fast water
160.8	Rattlesnake Bar	R	L	High bank
160.8	Magpie Creek	L	L	High water
160.0	Hida Creek	L	S	Low water - boulders
158.6	Bargamin Creek	R	L	High water - boulders
157.6	Bailey Creek	R	S	Low water - fast
156.9	Allison Ranch - Myers Creek	R	M	Low water
154.1	Richardson Creek - upper	L	S-L	Large upper bench Low water boulder beach

Main Salmon River Camps

River Mile	Name	Left or Right Bank	Camp Size Small, Medium, Large	Comment
153.9	Yellow Pine Bar - Camp Creek	R	L	High water
154.0	Yellow Pine Bar - lower	R	M	High water
153.5	Big Mallard Creek	R	L	High water
152.5	Twin Snags	L	M	High water - rocky bank
152.4	Deep Hole	R	L	High water
151.7	Hermit Hanks	L	L	High rocky bank
151.0	Several small low water beaches below whitewater ranch			
149.2	Little Trout Creek	L	S	High rocky bank
149.1	Growler	R	S	Fast water
148.1	Pebble Beach	L	S	1/4 mile below bridge
147.8	Jim Moore -			
	(Lower Campbell's Ferry)	R	L	1/2 mile below bridge
147.6	Ruff Creek	L	S	Low water
147.1	Groundhog Bar	R	L	High water
145.7	Hancock Bar - upper	R	S	
145.4	Hancock Bar - lower	R	L	High water
144.0	Rhett Creek	R	L	High water - rocky bank
141.4	Paine Creek	R	M	Low water
	Two low water beaches between Paine Creek - Boise Bar			
140.0	Boise Bar	R	M	Low water
139.2	No Man Creek	R	S	Low water
138.7	Tepee Creek	R	S	Low water
138.0	Buckskin Bill's (5 Mile Creek)			No camping
138.0	5 Mile Creek - lower	L	M	
137.5	Klondike Bar (Haney Bar)	L	L	Low water - rocky landing
137.0	Blue Bird Hole	R	L	One mile below Buckskin Bill's, high water bar
135.1	Mackay Bar Bridge	R	L	At bridge
133.9	South Fork Salmon	L	L	Access upper channel of Island on South Fork
133.9	South Fork Island	L	M	Low water Lower end of Island
133.5	Chukar Bar	L	S	Low water
132.6	Cove Creek - lower	R	S	1/4 mile below Cove Creek Low water
131.8	No Name Beach	L	S	Low water
129.8	Hungry Bar	R	M	Low water
129.7	Mann Creek	L	L	High water
129.4	Warren Creek	L	L	High water - rocky
129.2	Warren Bar	R	L	High water - sand beach
128.3	Indian Creek	R	L	High bank, difficult camp access
127.8	James Creek - Ranch	L	S	
125.3	Rabbit Creek	L	M	Low water
123.8	Dry Bar	L	M	
122.7	Basin Creek	R	M	Low water
122.0	Whiskey Bob Creek	R	M	High water
121.1	Bull Creek - upper	R	L	Low water - no shade
120.9	Bull Creek - lower	R	L	High water
119.5	Gold Rush Bar	R	S	High water

River Mile	Name	Left or Right Bank	Camp Size Small, Medium, Large	Comment
119.4	California Creek	L	L	Low water, fast water
118.9	T-Bone Creek	R	M	Low water
117.7	Maxwell Bar	L	L	Low water
116.7	Sheep Creek	R	M	High water - horse corral
116.4	Rams Horn Bar	L	S	
115.3	Dried Meat	R	S	Before Dried Meat Rapids
114.8	Slide Beach	L	S	1/2 mile below Dried Meat Rap.
114.5	Johnson Creek	R	S	High water
113.7	Bear Creek	L	S	
112.6	Long Tom Creek	L	M	Rocky bank
111.8	Vinegar Creek	L		Boat ramp
109.8	Wind River Bridge	R	L	Under bridge
109.7	Carey Creek - boat ramp	L		Boat ramp - waste disposal

*High or low water refers to approximately over or under 10,000 c.f.s. flow at Corn Creek launch. High water camps are useable at high flows while low water camps may not be useable at high flows.

THE MAIN SALMON "RIVER OF NO RETURN" LOG

River mile: 191 to 112 . . . . 79 miles

Drift time: 17 hours . . . . 4.7 m.p.h.

Logged in raft

River classification: Expert

River drop: 12 feet per mile average

River discharge: 3,000-3,300 c.f.s. Corn Creek gage

Information: permits, shuttle service, river flow

North Fork Ranger District

P.O. Box 180

North Fork, Idaho 83466

(208) 865-2700

Lottery permit applications December 1 through January 31.

Permits required all year.

Lottery permit season June 20 through September 7.

MAIN SALMON RIVER
CORN CREEK GAGE
RIVER MILE 190

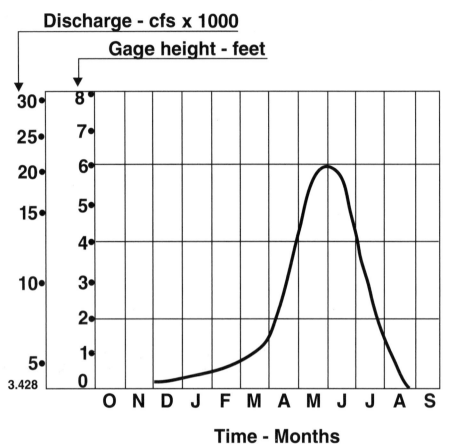

Discharge - cfs x 1000

Gage height - feet

Time - Months

Hazard

Low - under 5,000 cfs
Moderate - 5,000-10,000 cfs
High - over 10,000 cfs

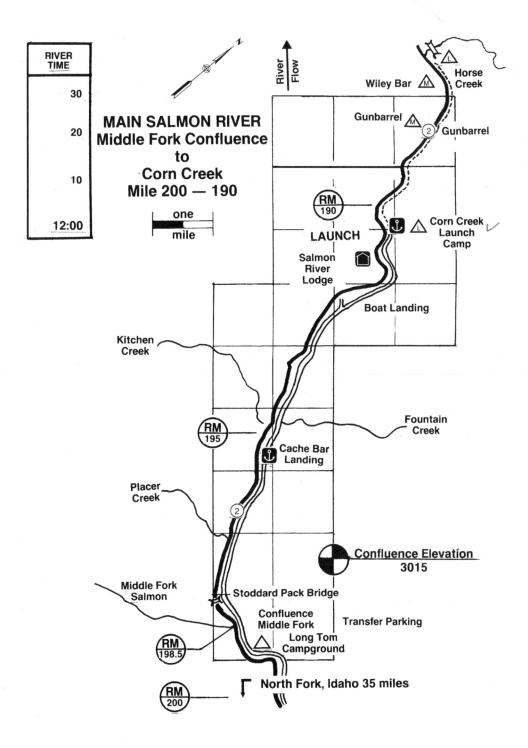

RIVER TIME

30

20

10

12:00

MAIN SALMON RIVER
Middle Fork Confluence
to
Corn Creek
Mile 200 — 190

one
mile

River Flow

Horse Creek

Wiley Bar

Gunbarrel

Gunbarrel

RM 190

LAUNCH

Corn Creek Launch Camp

Salmon River Lodge

Boat Landing

Kitchen Creek

Fountain Creek

RM 195

Cache Bar Landing

Placer Creek

Confluence Elevation
3015

Middle Fork Salmon

Stoddard Pack Bridge

Confluence Middle Fork

Transfer Parking

Long Tom Campground

RM 198.5

North Fork, Idaho 35 miles

RM 200

83

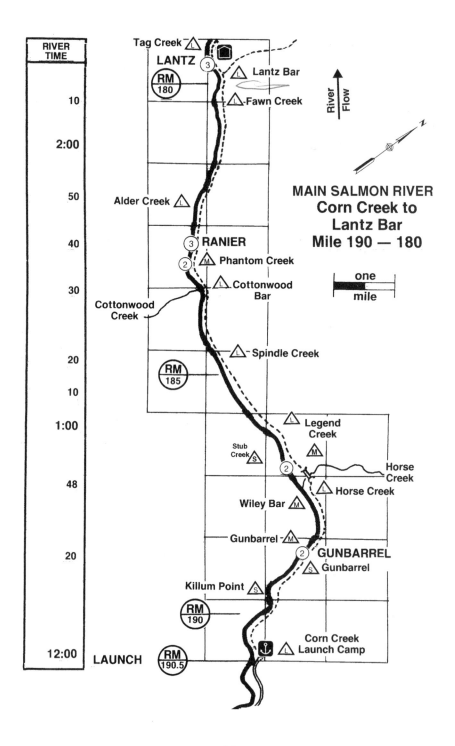

RIVER TIME

MAIN SALMON RIVER
Corn Creek to
Lantz Bar
Mile 190 — 180

one mile

Tag Creek

LANTZ

RM 180

Lantz Bar

Fawn Creek

2:00

50

Alder Creek

40

RANIER

Phantom Creek

30

Cottonwood Bar

Cottonwood Creek

20

Spindle Creek

RM 185

10

1:00

Legend Creek

Stub Creek

Horse Creek

48

Horse Creek

Wiley Bar

Gunbarrel

20

GUNBARREL

Gunbarrel

Killum Point

RM 190

RM 190.5

12:00 **LAUNCH**

Corn Creek Launch Camp

84

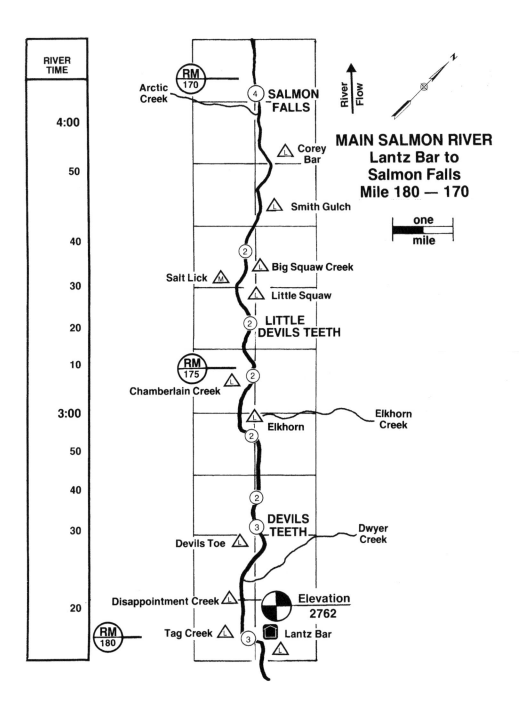

RIVER TIME

4:00
50
40
30
20
10
3:00
50
40
30
20

RM 170
Arctic Creek
SALMON FALLS (4)

Corey Bar

Smith Gulch

Big Squaw Creek (2)

Salt Lick

Little Squaw

LITTLE DEVILS TEETH (2)

RM 175
Chamberlain Creek (2)

Elkhorn (2)
Elkhorn Creek

(2)

DEVILS TEETH (3)
Dwyer Creek

Devils Toe

Disappointment Creek

Elevation 2762

Tag Creek (3)
Lantz Bar

RM 180

MAIN SALMON RIVER
Lantz Bar to
Salmon Falls
Mile 180 — 170

River Flow

one mile

85

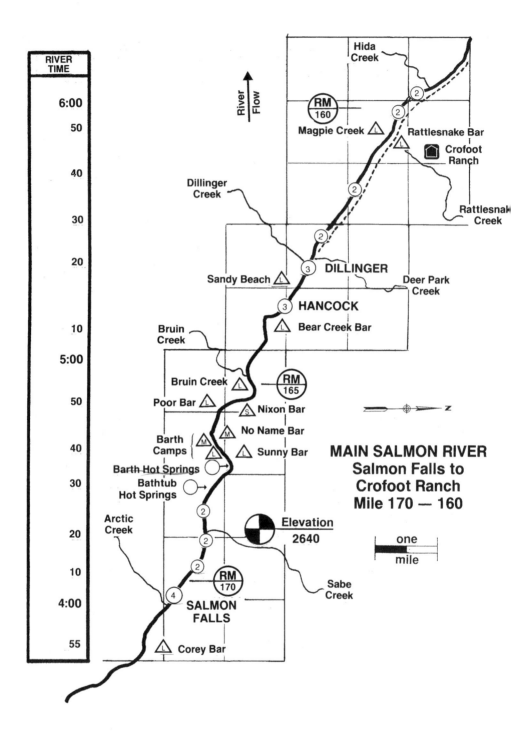

RIVER TIME

6:00
50
40
30
20
10
5:00
50
40
30
20
10
4:00
55

Hida Creek

River Flow

RM 160

Magpie Creek ⚠

Rattlesnake Bar

Crofoot Ranch

Dillinger Creek

Rattlesnak Creek

Sandy Beach ⚠

DILLINGER

Deer Park Creek

HANCOCK

Bruin Creek

Bear Creek Bar

Bruin Creek ⚠

RM 165

Poor Bar ⚠

Nixon Bar

No Name Bar

Barth Camps

Sunny Bar

Barth Hot Springs

Bathtub Hot Springs

Arctic Creek

Elevation 2640

MAIN SALMON RIVER
Salmon Falls to
Crofoot Ranch
Mile 170 — 160

one mile

Sabe Creek

RM 170

SALMON FALLS

⚠ Corey Bar

86

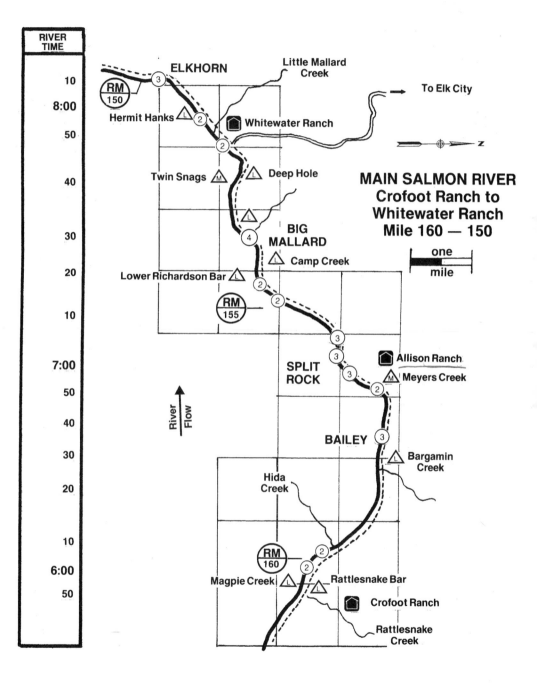

RIVER TIME

10
8:00
50
40
30
20
10
7:00
50
40
30
20
10
6:00
50

RM 150

ELKHORN

Little Mallard Creek

To Elk City

Hermit Hanks

Whitewater Ranch

Twin Snags

Deep Hole

MAIN SALMON RIVER
Crofoot Ranch to
Whitewater Ranch
Mile 160 — 150

one
mile

BIG MALLARD

Camp Creek

Lower Richardson Bar

RM 155

SPLIT ROCK

Allison Ranch

Meyers Creek

River Flow

BAILEY

Bargamin Creek

Hida Creek

RM 160

Magpie Creek

Rattlesnake Bar

Crofoot Ranch

Rattlesnake Creek

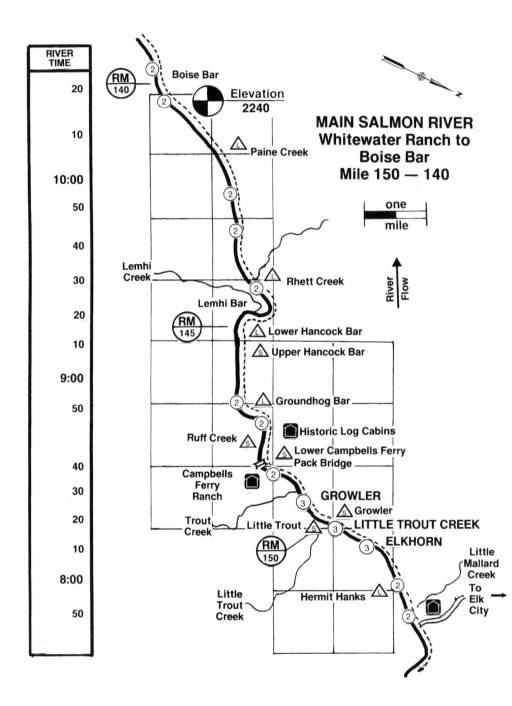

RIVER TIME

20
10
10:00
50
40
30
20
10
9:00
50
40
30
20
10
8:00
50

RM 140
Boise Bar
Elevation 2240

MAIN SALMON RIVER
Whitewater Ranch to
Boise Bar
Mile 150 — 140

one mile

River Flow

L Paine Creek

Lemhi Creek
L Rhett Creek
Lemhi Bar
RM 145
L Lower Hancock Bar
S Upper Hancock Bar

L Groundhog Bar
Historic Log Cabins
Ruff Creek S
S Lower Campbells Ferry
Pack Bridge
Campbells Ferry Ranch
GROWLER
S Growler
Trout Creek
Little Trout S
LITTLE TROUT CREEK
RM 150
ELKHORN
Little Mallard Creek
To Elk City
Little Trout Creek
Hermit Hanks L

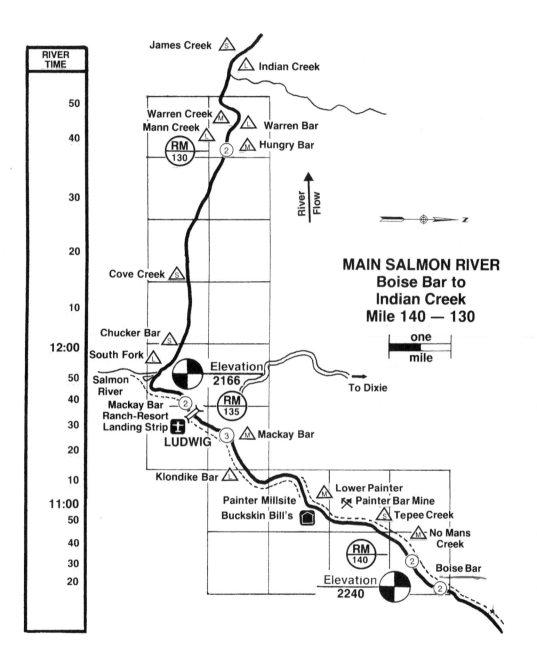

RIVER TIME

James Creek ⟨S⟩
⟨L⟩ Indian Creek

50
Warren Creek ⟨M⟩
Mann Creek ⟨L⟩ ⟨L⟩ Warren Bar
40
RM 130 ② ⟨M⟩ Hungry Bar

30

River Flow

MAIN SALMON RIVER
Boise Bar to
Indian Creek
Mile 140 — 130

20

Cove Creek ⟨S⟩

10

one
mile

Chucker Bar ⟨S⟩
12:00
South Fork ⟨L⟩
Elevation 2166
50 Salmon River
To Dixie
40 Mackay Bar ②
Ranch-Resort RM 135
30 Landing Strip ✚ ③ ⟨M⟩ Mackay Bar
LUDWIG
20

10 Klondike Bar ⟨L⟩
Lower Painter
11:00 ⟨M⟩ ⚒ Painter Bar Mine
50 Painter Millsite
Buckskin Bill's ⌂ ⟨S⟩ Tepee Creek
40 ⟨M⟩ No Mans Creek
30 RM 140 ②
20 Elevation 2240 Boise Bar
②

89

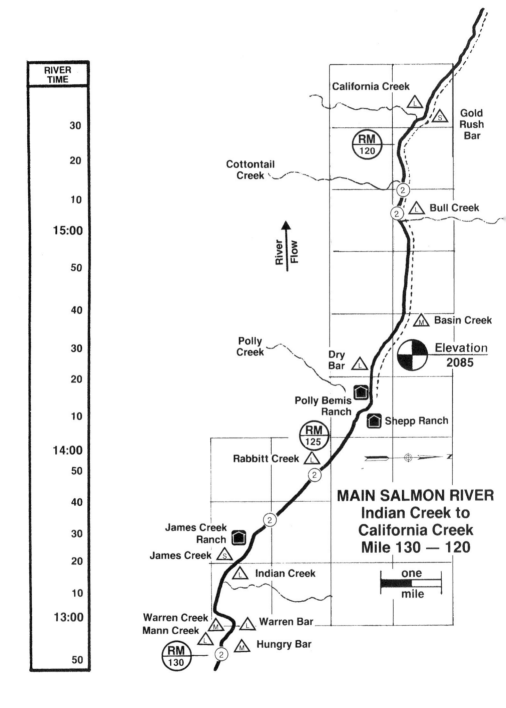

RIVER TIME

30
20
10
15:00
50
40
30
20
10
14:00
50
40
30
20
10
13:00
50

California Creek

Gold Rush Bar

RM 120

Cottontail Creek

River Flow

Bull Creek

Basin Creek

Polly Creek

Dry Bar

Elevation 2085

Polly Bemis Ranch

Shepp Ranch

RM 125

Rabbitt Creek

MAIN SALMON RIVER
Indian Creek to
California Creek
Mile 130 — 120

James Creek Ranch

James Creek

one mile

Indian Creek

Warren Creek
Mann Creek

Warren Bar

RM 130

Hungry Bar

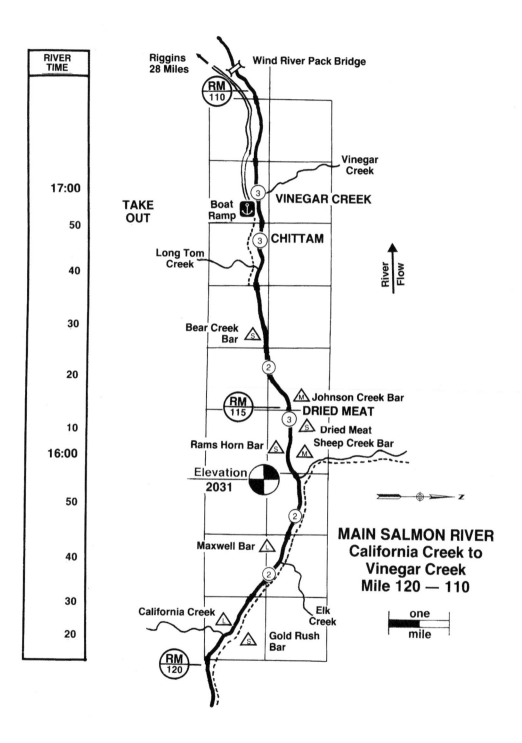

RIVER TIME

Riggins 28 Miles

Wind River Pack Bridge

RM 110

Vinegar Creek

17:00

TAKE OUT

Boat Ramp ⚓

③ VINEGAR CREEK

50

③ CHITTAM

Long Tom Creek

40

River Flow

30

Bear Creek Bar ⛰ S

20

②

RM 115

⛰ M Johnson Creek Bar

DRIED MEAT

10

③ ⛰ S Dried Meat

16:00

Rams Horn Bar ⛰ S

⛰ M Sheep Creek Bar

Elevation 2031

50

②

z

40

Maxwell Bar ⛰ L

MAIN SALMON RIVER
California Creek to
Vinegar Creek
Mile 120 — 110

②

30

California Creek ⛰

Elk Creek

one
mile

20

⛰ S Gold Rush Bar

RM 120

91

Green Canyon — R.M. 48-41

The Lower Salmon River

Whitebird, Idaho to Confluence with
Snake River and Continuing to
Mouth of Grande Ronde River

The Salmon River has its origins north of the famous ski resort of Sun Valley, Idaho, near Galena Summit centered in Idaho's Sawtooth Mountains. The river runs northeasterly toward Idaho's eastern border at North Fork, Idaho, then it turns abruptly westward cutting across Idaho to Riggins on the western border. From Riggins the river runs northwesterly to its confluence with the Snake River. Within this 425-mile circuitous journey, there are many places for boating. The more popular are from Corn Creek, near the Middle Fork of the Salmon confluence with the Main Salmon, to Vinegar Creek about 28 miles upstream from Riggins. This is called the "Main Salmon" or "River of No Return Section." The Middle Fork of the Salmon, a major tributary, is also a popular trip. This log is for the Lower Salmon section starting at Whitebird, Idaho, and continuing 54 miles to the confluence with the Snake River and then 20 additional miles on the Snake to the mouth of the Grande Ronde River, for a total trip length of 74 miles.

For boaters familiar with the "Middle Fork" or "Main Salmon" trips, this section is distinctly different. The elevation change for the "Lower Salmon" is from 1,426 to 905, while the other popular trips mentioned start at an elevation over 5,700 feet at Dagger Falls on the Middle Fork or 3,015 feet at the confluence of the Middle Fork with the Main Salmon. This trip is in a treeless, semi-arid desert environment and a large canyon similar to, but slightly smaller in scale to, the lower Snake River section of "Hells Canyon." The Salmon River forms the deepest gorge next to Hells Canyon of the Snake River on the continent. There are four rugged canyon sections on the Lower Salmon called Green, Cougar, Snowhole and Blue Canyons.

This section of the Salmon has many large, beautiful sandy beaches which lure one into a false complacency about camp frequency. There are several sections, particularly the canyon sections, where there are few camps except for small, unparticular parties willing to spend the night in a special canyon niche. Even the large sandy beach camps may have shade limitations, and straying from the river can expose the boater to high temperatures, snake habitat and poison ivy.

The most popular river boating flows are below 10,000 c.f.s. with preferable flows of 5,000-10,000 c.f.s. At high flows above 15,000 c.f.s. Slide Rapids at river mile 3 becomes an extremely difficult rapids. An informal river hazard rating has been developed for the Lower Salmon similar to the Main Salmon "River of No Return." Under 5,000 c.f.s. low, 5,000-10,000 moderate and over 10,000 c.f.s. high hazard. The popular boating flows ordinarily occur in August, assuring a high probability for 90°+ Fahrenheit temperatures. Fortunately, the low humidity, river breezes and low night temperatures make the trip tolerable even for heat sensitive people. The river is relatively warm, which lends itself to swimming in August and is an aid to keeping cool on hot days.

The character of the rapids is distinctly pool and drop. The majority of rapids are Class 1, 2 and 3 with one Class 4 (Snow-Hole rapids). The rapids rating depends primarily on river flow, but, excepting Snow-Hole rapids, this is essentially a big water Class 3 river. The average river slope is 10 feet per mile, suggesting that river velocity between rapids, at moderate flows, will be on the order of 4 m.p.h.

During our trip we encountered many chukars which seem to thrive in this arid, rocky canyon environment. We noticed some ducks and two otters that playfully foreran a set of rapids with us. We did not notice a great deal of wildlife, but then observing animals is an accumulated skill depending on many things. Certainly we must miss the majority of wildlife that obviously exists along the water's way. There are primitive roads, ranches and other signs of civilization during some of the trip. Wilderness river trips rarely exist except possibly in the upper regions of some remote rivers. The Lower Salmon comes about as close as possible because of the present limited boating use. This, unfortunately, is quickly changing as the national advertising campaigns get underway to attract more people to this section of the river. Thus far, reservation type permits for this section are not required.

The main deterrent to this trip is the last 20 miles on the Snake with the heavy power boat use, upriver winds and almost total lack of whitewater. Power boats run the full length of the Salmon from Whitebird to the confluence. Rarely, however, have we encountered power boats on our Lower Salmon river trips. Most of the power boats will be encountered on the Snake River. This trip is sometimes coupled with a trip on the upper section of Hells Canyon by

Cougar Canyon — R.M. 32-27

Snow Hole Rapids — R.M. 23

Lower Salmon River Canyon — R.M. 8

Greg Smith

exiting from the Snake River at Pittsburg landing, then shuttling out of the Snake River Canyon into the Salmon River Canyon at Whitebird.

A combined trip such as this can be handled as a single shuttle. With proper timing, shuttle drivers can meet boaters at Pittsburg landing, then shuttle to Whitebird and continue to Hellers Bar near the mouth of the Grande Ronde on the Snake River. There are, of course, endless shuttle strategies for the boater to consider. This two river trip combines the best of the Snake River (Hells Canyon Dam to Johnsons Bar) with the rare desert beauty of the Lower Salmon. Other combinations exist for coordinating this trip with the Selway, Middle Fork or Main Salmon Rivers. It is unnecessary to combine this trip with any other except for convenience because the Lower Salmon River is worthwhile entirely on its own merits.

Lower Salmon River Campsites

River Mile	Name	Left or Right Bank	Camp Size Small, Medium, Large	Comments
52	Hammer Creek	L	L	Developed Camp
50	Lyons Bar Area	L	L	Three Large Sites
46	Woodruff Gulch	L & R	L	Two Large Sites Left and Right
45	Shorts Bar	L	S,L	Two Sites, Pictographs Across River at Shorts Bar
42	Pine Bar	R	L	Developed Camp
41	Lone Pine Bar	L	L	Two Sites
33	Packers Creek Area	R	L	Several Large Sites, Last Large Sites for Five Miles
27	White House Bar	R	L	Three Large Sites, Last Large Sites for Eight Miles
20	Maloney Creek	R	L	Two Large Sites, One Above and One Below Creek
18-16	Billy Creek Area			Seven Large Camps this Area
13	Eagle Creek Area	R	L	Several Large Campsites
10-8	Skeleton Creek - Wapshilla Area	L	L	Several Large Sites

River Mile	Name	Left or Right Bank	Camp Size Small, Medium, Large	Comments
				Two Large Camps Left and Right, Few Camps Next
6	Blue Canyon	L & R	L	Five Miles
2	Buzzards Roost	L	L	Heavy Jet Boat Use
1	Pullman Mine	L	L	
0	Confluence Sites	R	L	Two Large Sites

See Hells Canyon of the Snake River campsites for camps below confluence.

LOWER SALMON RIVER
WHITEBIRD GAGE
RIVER MILE 54

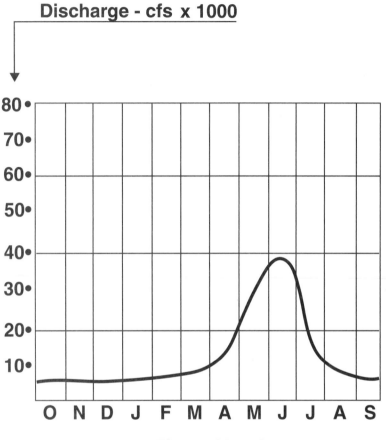

Discharge - cfs x 1000

Time - Months

Hazard

Low - under 5,000 cfs
Moderate - 5,000-10,000 cfs
High - over 10,000 cfs

LOWER SALMON RIVER LOG

Whitebird, Idaho to Confluence with Snake River
and Continuing to Mouth of Grande Ronde River

River mile: 54 to 0 on Salmon

188 to 168 on Snake . . . . Total 74 miles

Drift time: 21 hours 35 minutes . . . . 3.3 m.p.h.

Logged in raft

River classification: Expert

River drop: 10 feet per mile average

River discharge: 3,600 c.f.s. Whitebird gage

Recommended discharge: 5,000-10,000

River discharge information:

Boise National Weather Service (208) 334-9860

Information: shuttle service

U.S. Bureau of Land Management

Route 3, Box 181

Cottonwood, Idaho 83522

(208) 962-3245

No river permit or camp assignments required.

Self-issuing information permits requested at

Hammer Creek launch.

LEGEND

MAP SYMBOLS

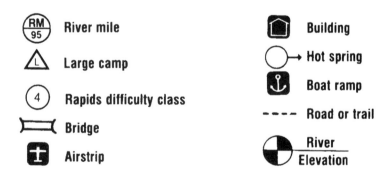

(RM 95) River mile		Building
(L) Large camp		Hot spring
(4) Rapids difficulty class		Boat ramp
Bridge		Road or trail
Airstrip		River Elevation

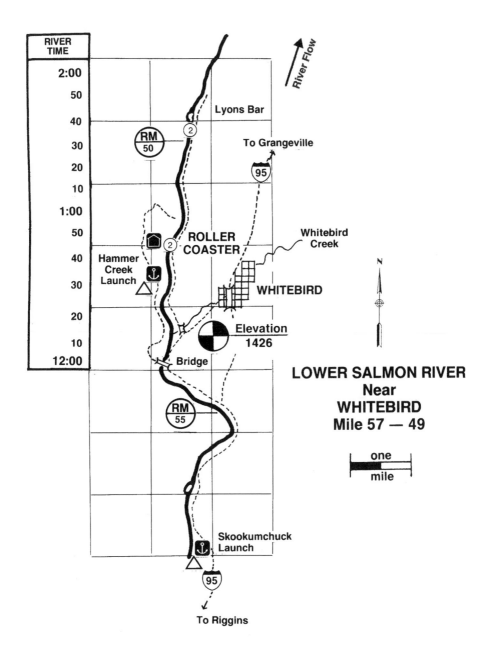

RIVER TIME

2:00
50
40
30
20
10
1:00
50
40
30
20
10
12:00

Lyons Bar

RM 50

2

To Grangeville

95

ROLLER COASTER

Whitebird Creek

Hammer Creek Launch

WHITEBIRD

Elevation 1426

Bridge

RM 55

N

LOWER SALMON RIVER
Near
WHITEBIRD
Mile 57 — 49

one
mile

Skookumchuck Launch

95

To Riggins

River Flow

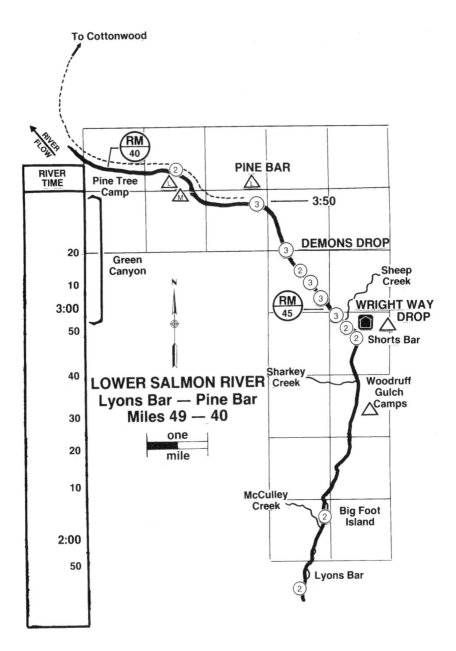

To Cottonwood

RIVER FLOW

RIVER TIME

RM 40

Pine Tree Camp

② L

PINE BAR

② L

③ —— 3:50

DEMONS DROP

③

20

Green Canyon

② ③ ③

Sheep Creek

10

RM 45

③

WRIGHT WAY DROP

3:00

50

② ②

Shorts Bar

40

Sharkey Creek

Woodruff Gulch Camps

LOWER SALMON RIVER
Lyons Bar — Pine Bar
Miles 49 — 40

30

one

20

mile

10

McCulley Creek

② Big Foot Island

2:00

50

Lyons Bar

②

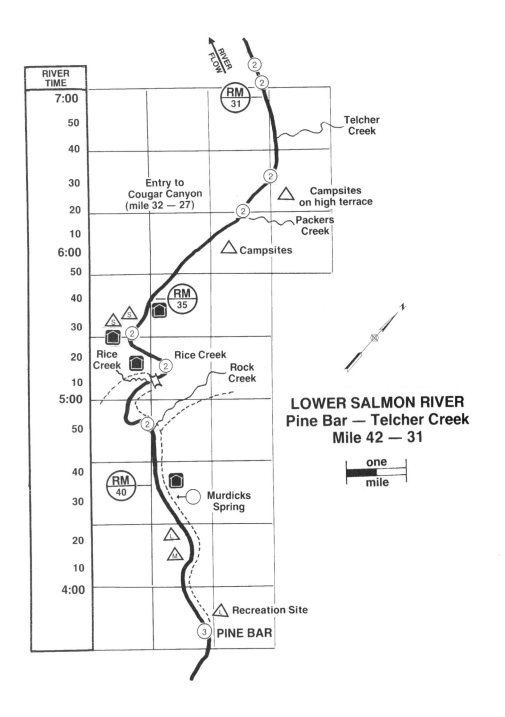

RIVER TIME

7:00
50
40
30
20
10
6:00
50
40
30
20
10
5:00
50
40
30
20
10
4:00

RIVER FLOW

② ②

RM 31

Telcher Creek

Entry to Cougar Canyon (mile 32 — 27)

② Campsites on high terrace

②

Packers Creek

△ Campsites

RM 35

△S △S

② Rice Creek

Rice Creek

Rock Creek

②

RM 40

○ Murdicks Spring

△L

△M

△L Recreation Site

③ **PINE BAR**

LOWER SALMON RIVER
Pine Bar — Telcher Creek
Mile 42 — 31

one mile

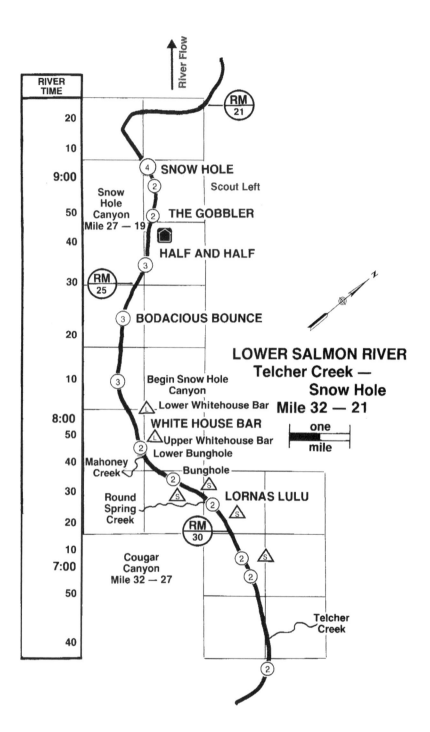

River Flow

RIVER TIME

RM 21

20
10

9:00 ④ **SNOW HOLE** Scout Left
②

Snow Hole Canyon Mile 27 — 19

50 ② **THE GOBBLER**
40

③ **HALF AND HALF**

RM 25

30

③ **BODACIOUS BOUNCE**

20

LOWER SALMON RIVER
Telcher Creek —
Snow Hole
Mile 32 — 21

10 ③ Begin Snow Hole Canyon
△ Lower Whitehouse Bar

8:00 **WHITE HOUSE BAR** one
50 △L Upper Whitehouse Bar mile
② Lower Bunghole
40 Mahoney Creek Bunghole
30 ② Bunghole △S
Round Spring Creek △S **LORNAS LULU**
20 ② △S
RM 30
10 ② △S
7:00 Cougar Canyon Mile 32 — 27
②
50

Telcher Creek

40

②

104

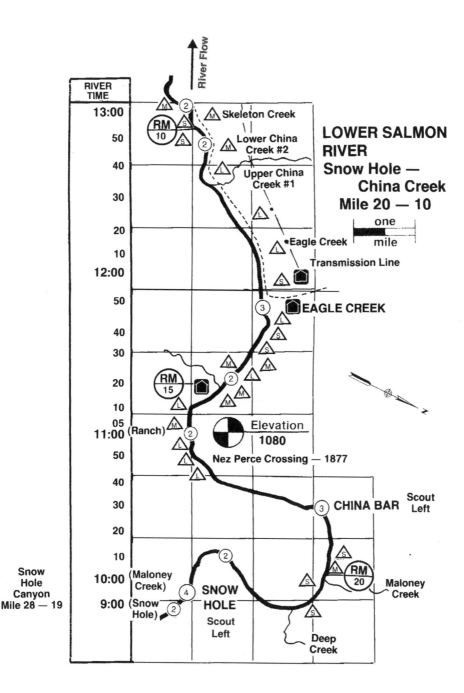

River Flow

RIVER TIME	
13:00	

RM 10

Skeleton Creek

Lower China Creek #2

Upper China Creek #1

LOWER SALMON RIVER
Snow Hole —
China Creek
Mile 20 — 10

one mile

Eagle Creek

Transmission Line

EAGLE CREEK

RM 15

Elevation **1080**

(Ranch)

Nez Perce Crossing — 1877

CHINA BAR Scout Left

RM 20

Maloney Creek

(Maloney Creek)

SNOW HOLE

Scout Left

(Snow Hole)

Deep Creek

Snow Hole Canyon Mile 28 — 19

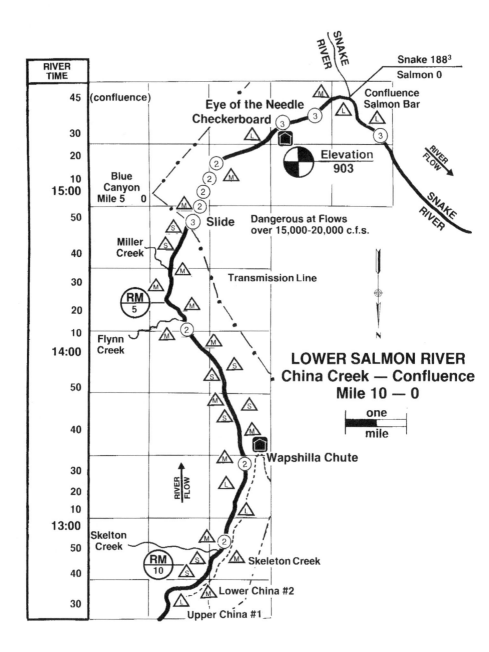

LOWER SALMON RIVER
China Creek — Confluence
Mile 10 — 0

RIVER TIME

45 (confluence)
30
20
10
15:00
50
40
30
20
10
14:00
50
40
30
20
10
13:00
50
40
30

Snake 188³
Salmon 0

Confluence
Salmon Bar

Eye of the Needle
Checkerboard

Elevation
903

Blue
Canyon
Mile 5   0

Slide   Dangerous at Flows
over 15,000-20,000 c.f.s.

Miller
Creek

Transmission Line

RM
5

Flynn
Creek

one
mile

Wapshilla Chute

RIVER
FLOW

Skelton
Creek

RM
10

Skeleton Creek

Lower China #2

Upper China #1

RIVER
FLOW

SNAKE
RIVER

RIVER
FLOW

SNAKE
RIVER

Greg Smith

Hells Canyon at Saddle Creek — R.M. 236

Hells Canyon of the Snake River
Hells Canyon Dam to Grande Ronde River

The Snake River originates just north of Jackson Lake, Wyoming near the Yellowstone Park southern boundary. From Wyoming the river carves its way through southern Idaho, providing power and irrigation in an agricultural area that would otherwise be desert. The duties of the Snake were clearly defined many years ago. After making Southern Idaho bloom from irrigation, it would provide an entire series of dams through the non-agricultural Hells Canyon. These dams were planned in a manner that would make the Snake a contiguous group of lakes, linking dam forebay to dam tailrace and harnessing this river in what was just one resource in an entire development plan for the Columbia River Basin. The Snake River is over 1,000 miles long, winding through four states and draining an area larger than the state of Idaho. Anyone could see its potential energy and importance to the West.

It became a matter of not whether to develop this resource, but how. Engineers and politicians wrangled for years over such technical problems as High Sheep Dam vs. Low Sheep Dam. While this controversy was taking place in the design rooms, political arenas and courts, the public mood was changing to a course of action no one had originally considered seriously — the no-build option. Americans can credit former Justice William O. Douglas with his famous decision that was instrumental in paving the way for no more dams within Hells Canyon. In essence, Justice Douglas ordered the Federal Power Commission to rehear the entire case with adequate consideration to be given to the question of whether or not there should be any dam at all. That isn't what the power company litigants in the Supreme Court decision had in mind. The National Wild and Scenic Rivers Act of 1968 was the forerunner of later acts that would protect Hells Canyon in its free flowing natural state. In 1975 the National Recreation Act was signed into law, and a 31-mile section of the Snake River, between Hells Canyon Dam and Pittsburg Landing, became a wild section of the National Wild and Scenic River System. The 36-mile section from River Mile 180.1 to Pittsburg Landing has been designated a Scenic River.

To many boaters, the most outstanding section is the first 17 miles from Hells Canyon to Johnsons Bar. This is the most interesting from any view, scenery, wilderness or rapids. By measuring from the top of 9,400 foot Seven Devils Mountains on the Idaho side or rugged peaks on the Oregon side, you come up with the fact that this is the deepest canyon on the North American continent. Hells Canyon is majestic by any standard, whether it be looking up from the river or a mile down from Hat Point on the Oregon side.

Starting your trip from the Hells Canyon Dam boat launch, you go only five miles downstream before you come to the first class five rapids on the tour — Wild Sheep Creek Rapids. We always scout this rapids and have run it on the left (Oregon tongue), the center and the right (Idaho side). It depends mainly on your skill, equipment and attitude where to run it, so scout and decide. I have run Wild Sheep in the small rafts, affectionately called "The Yellow Peril," and friends of mine have run it in open canoes.

The next, and only other, class five rapids is Granite Falls. We always scout on the left and usually run on the left, or Oregon side, although there is a route on the Idaho side also. Again, members of our party have run it left, right and down the center. Anyone who runs this rapids down the center, excepting possibly the large commercial rafts, is asking for trouble. I never intended to run the center into the huge hole; it was just an error and something never forgotten. Granite has my attention and respect. At most river stages it is a lot of whitewater in a short distance. Although Wild Sheep and Granite are class five rapids, they could both be portaged fairly easily by kayakers, but rafts would have a difficult time, which is probably the reason most boaters run both these rapids after scouting.

There are three class three rapids at Bernard Creek that provide excitement, yet we do not scout them. We do scout Waterspout and Rush Creek when new boaters are along. Waterspout is deceptive because there is a large rock left of center near the end of the rapids that can flip most any raft. The deception is the current which actually draws boaters into this hazard, and I suspect the number of boaters "flipping" in Waterspout approaches the number for Wild Sheep Creek Rapids. It is apparent which route to take at Rush Creek if you scout, or at least can read water reasonably well.

The upper section from Hells Canyon Dam to Johnsons Bar is my favorite part of the river. That is where the rapids, wildlife and scenery are, and by comparison to the lower sections, it is more of a wilderness experience. Actually, power boats run the full length of the river. As a practical matter, the power tourist boats run downstream from the Dam to Wild Sheep Creek Rapids. Other power boats run unrestricted upstream to Granite Creek. These two rapids form a natural barrier to most power boats, leaving less than two miles between them free of power boats in this wild section.

Most of the camps in the upper section are on benches above the river. The shoreline is rocky with few sandy beaches and sometimes difficult landings. Dam discharges may fluctuate widely, requiring that boats be tied at a high elevation. We have been on the river when discharge varied between 5,000-20,000 c.f.s. in one day.

This can easily be a river elevation change of four feet and can significantly change some rapids. In climbing to high elevation camps, watch for poison ivy; it is all over. In August it is usually a temptation to sleep in the dry, open starlight, but we recently have adopted the practice of sleeping only in tents. We were startled one night by a rattlesnake only an arm's length from our open bed.

Boaters on the Snake compete for camps with other river corridor users including hikers, horse packers, and power boaters. The potential for camp conflicts exist, particularly below Granite Creek and Johnsons Bar. It is best to have alternate camps in mind.

The first exit point from the river is Pittsburg Landing on the Idaho side. The next exit is Dug Bar downstream on the Oregon side. The Imnaha Canyon shuttle into Dug Bar is through outstanding scenery, but is difficult so that few people exit there. The majority of people terminate their trip at Hellers Bar near the mouth of the Grande Ronde River. Pittsburg Landing is the terminus of the Wild River section and is convenient as an exit for Idaho people and for those combining Hells Canyon with the Lower Salmon trip. An increasing number of private boaters exit at Pittsburg to avoid the power boats with their camp conflicts, and because the remainder of the trip to Hellers Bar is noted for its upriver wind and lack of whitewater. Should you combine this tour with a Lower Salmon River trip, you will experience the last 20 miles of the trip on the Snake from the confluence of the Salmon to Hellers Bar near the mouth of the Grande Ronde River.

The designated Wild River section from Hells Canyon Dam to Kirby Creek (R.M. 221) just before Pittsburg Landing, has certain days when power boats are prohibited. The schedule can be obtained from the Forest Service-Hells Canyon National Recreation Area.

Greg Smith

111

SNAKE RIVER
HELLS CANYON DAM GAGE
RIVER MILE 248

Discharge - cfs x 1000
40,000
30,000
20,000
10,000
O N D J F M A M J J A S
Time - Months

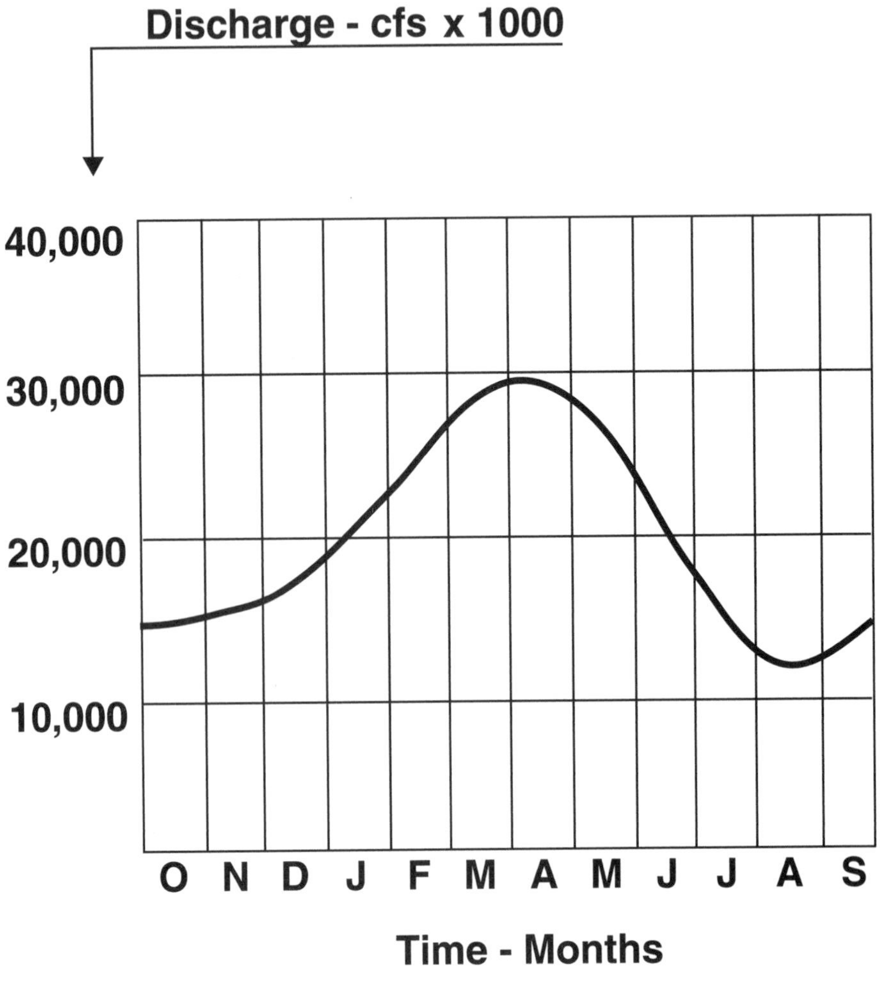

SHUTTLE MAP
GRANDE RONDE - SNAKE RIVERS

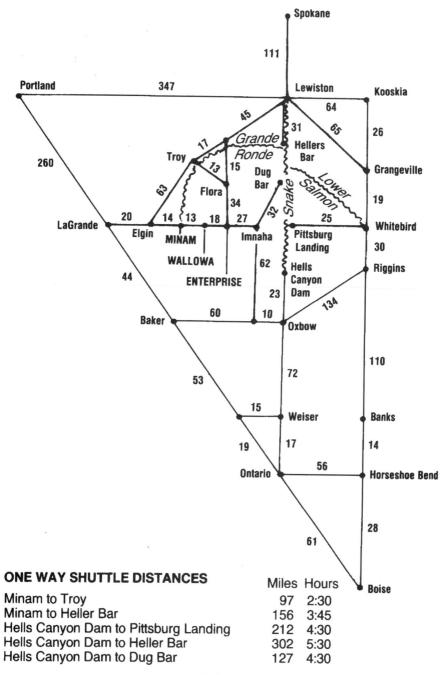

ONE WAY SHUTTLE DISTANCES	Miles	Hours
Minam to Troy	97	2:30
Minam to Heller Bar	156	3:45
Hells Canyon Dam to Pittsburg Landing	212	4:30
Hells Canyon Dam to Heller Bar	302	5:30
Hells Canyon Dam to Dug Bar	127	4:30

Hells Canyon of the Snake River Campsites

River Mile	Name	Left or Right Bank	Camp Size Small, Medium, Large	Good Landing	Shade
247	Hells Canyon Recreation Site				
245.9	Stub Creek	L	L		•
245.8	Lamont Springs	R	L	•	
245.2	Square Beach	R	S	•	
244.7	Brush Creek	R	M	•	
243.7	Rocky Point	R	M		•
243.4	Chimney Bar	R	L		•
243.0	Warm Springs	R	L		•
242.1	Battle Creek	L	L	•	•
241.8	Sand Dunes	L	S	•	
241.5	Birch Springs	R	M		
241.2	Wild Sheep	L	L		
240.4	Rocky Bar	R	L		•
239.6	Upper Granite Creek	R	L		•
239.5	Lower Granite Creek	R	L		•
239.2	Cache Creek	L	L		
238.0	Three Creek	R	L		
237.8	Upper Oregon Hole	L	S		
237.7	Oregon Hole	L	L		
237.3	Upper Dry Gulch	R	L	•	•
237.0	Lower Dry Gulch	R	L	•	•
236.6	Hastings	R	M		
236.2	Saddle Creek	L	L		•
235.1	Bernard Creek	R	L	•	•
231.8	Sluice Creek	L	L		
231.4	Rush Creek	L	L		
229.9	Johnson Bar Landing	R	L	•	
229.4	Sheep Creek	R	L		
229.0	Steep Creek	R	M	•	
228.6	Yreka Bar	L	L		•
228.2	Upper Sand Creek	L	M		
227.9	Sand Creek—Admin.	L			
227.5	Pine Bar	R	L	•	•
226.5	Upper Quartz Creek	L	L		
226.2	Lower Quartz Creek	L	L	•	•
225.2	Caribou Creek	R	L	• (Rafts)	•
224.5	Dry Gulch	L	L	•	•
224.5	Big Bar	R	L		

River Mile	Name	Left or Right Bank	Camp Size Small, Medium, Large	Good Landing	Shade
224.2	Air Strip	R			
222.9	Hominy Bar	L	L	•	
222.6	Salt Creek	L	L	•	•
222.2	Two Corral Creek	L	L	•	•
222.0	Gracie Bar	R	L	•	•
221.6	Half Moon Bar	R	M	•	
221.0	Slaughter Gulch	L	L	•	
220.7	Kirkwood Historic Ranch	R			
220.3	Kirkwood Bar Camps	R	L		•
220.0	Yankee Bar	L	S	•	•
219.6	Russell Bar	R	L	• (Rafts)	•
218.3	Cat Gulch	R	M	•	•
217.0	Corral Creek	R	L		•
216.4	Fish Trap Bar	L	L	•	
216.3	Upper Pittsburg—6 sites	R	L	•	•
216.2	Camp	R	S	•	•
215.7	Wilson Eddy	L	L	•	•
214.9	Pittsburg Landing	R			
214.5	Pittsburg Campground	R	L	•	
213.3	Pleasant Valley—4 sites	R	L		•
212.4	Davis Creek	L	M	•	
212.0	McCarty Creek	L	M		
210.8	Big Canyon	R	L	•	•
210.4	Lower Big Canyon	R	S	•	
210.0	Somers Creek	L	L		•
209.8	Camp Creek	L	L		•
209.4	Tryon Creek	L	L	•	•
208.0	Lookout Creek	L	L		•
204.5	Bob Creek	L	L	•	•
201.9	Bar Creek	L	L		•
199.2	Deep Creek— Chinese Camp	L			
198.4	Robinson Gulch	L	L		•
198.1	Dug Creek	L	S		
196.6	Dug Bar Landing	L	M		
196.2	Dug Bar—road access	L	M		
194.0	Zig Zag	R	S	•	
193.2	Divide Creek	R	L		•

115

River Mile	Name	Left or Right Bank	Camp Size Small, Medium, Large	Good Landing	Shade
192.4	China Bar	L	L		
191.7	Imnaha	L	M		•
191.2	Fargo Camp (Eureka Bar)	L	L		
190.4	Knight Creek	L	L	•	•
188.3	Salmon Mouth	R	L	•	
188.0	Salmon Falls	R	L	•	
187.8	Salmon Bar	L	L	•	
185.9	Cave Cove	L	M	•	•
184.6	Geneva Bar	L	L	•	
183.4	Cook Creek	L	M	•	
183.0	Sentinel Rock	L	M	•	
182.0	Lower Jim Creek	L	L	•	•
181.8	Meat Hole	R	S	•	
181.5	Cactus Bar	R	M	•	
181.3	Upper Cottonwood Creek	R	L	•	•
180.9	Lower Cottonwood Creek	R	L	•	
179.9	Upper Cougar Bar	R	M	•	
178.6	Coon Hollow	L	L		•
178.2	Cochran Island	L	L	• (Rafts)	•
178.1	Garden Creek	L	S	•	•
177.7	Upper Cache Creek	L	L	•	
177.0	Cache Creek Ranch—Admin.				
176.8	Lower Cache Creek	L	S	•	
168.4	Heller Bar boat ramp				

SNAKE RIVER LOG
Hells Canyon Dam to Grande Ronde River

River mile: 247 to 168 . . . . Total 79 miles

Drift time: 20hours 30 minutes . . . . 4.0 m.p.h.

Logged in raft

River slope: 10 feet per mile average

River discharge: 10,000 to 12,000 c.f.s. Hells Canyon Dam

Recommended discharge: 15,000 c.f.s. maximum

River discharge information:

Hells Canyon Dam discharge

Idaho Power Company

1-800-422-3143 Idaho toll free

1-800-521-9102 Oregon toll free

Boise National Weather Service (208) 334-9860

Information: permits, shuttle service, river flow

Hells Canyon National Recreation Area

2535 Riverside Drive

P.O. Box 699

Clarkston, WA 99403

(509) 758-1957

1-888-758-8037 Toll free October 1 through end of February.

Lottery permit applications December 1 to January 31.

Primary reservation permit season, Friday before Memorial

Day through September 10.

Permits required all year.

LEGEND

MAP SYMBOLS

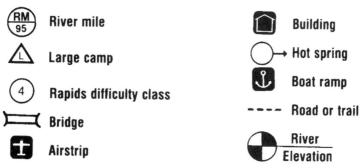

RM 95 — River mile

L — Large camp

4 — Rapids difficulty class

Bridge

Airstrip

Building

Hot spring

Boat ramp

Road or trail

River Elevation

Granite Falls Rapids — R.M. 239

Wild Sheep Creek Rapids — R.M. 241

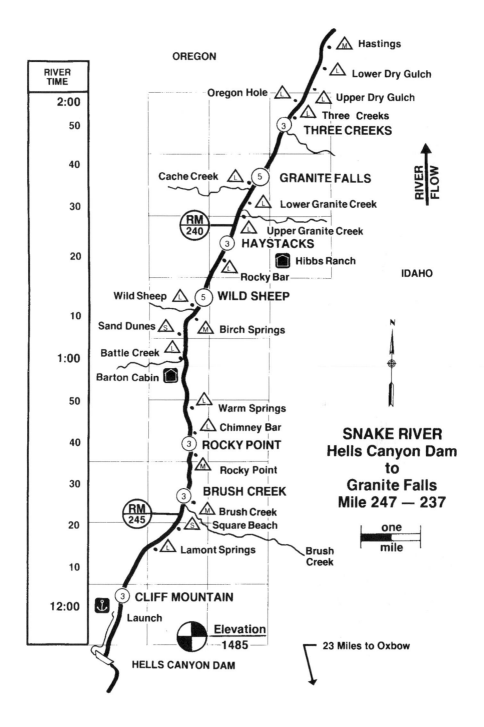

RIVER TIME

2:00
50
40
30
20
10
1:00
50
40
30
20
10
12:00

OREGON

Hastings
Lower Dry Gulch
Oregon Hole
Upper Dry Gulch
Three Creeks
THREE CREEKS
Cache Creek
GRANITE FALLS
Lower Granite Creek
RM 240
Upper Granite Creek
HAYSTACKS
Hibbs Ranch
Rocky Bar
IDAHO
Wild Sheep
WILD SHEEP
Sand Dunes
Birch Springs
Battle Creek
Barton Cabin
Warm Springs
Chimney Bar
ROCKY POINT
Rocky Point
BRUSH CREEK
RM 245
Brush Creek
Square Beach
Lamont Springs
Brush Creek
CLIFF MOUNTAIN
Launch

RIVER FLOW

N

SNAKE RIVER
Hells Canyon Dam
to
Granite Falls
Mile 247 — 237

one
mile

Elevation
1485

23 Miles to Oxbow

HELLS CANYON DAM

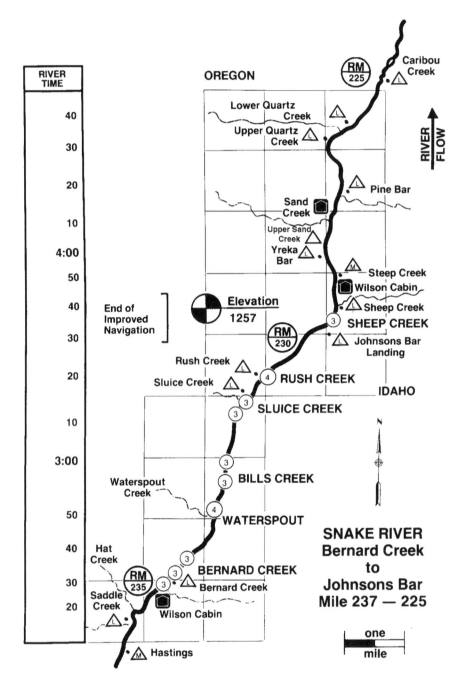

SNAKE RIVER
Bernard Creek
to
Johnsons Bar
Mile 237 — 225

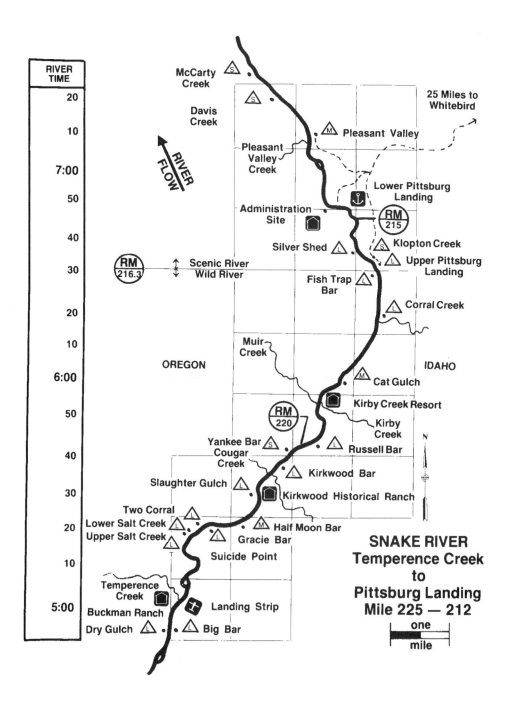

RIVER TIME

20
10
7:00
50
40
30
20
10
6:00
50
40
30
20
10
5:00

McCarty Creek

Davis Creek

25 Miles to Whitebird

Pleasant Valley

Pleasant Valley Creek

Lower Pittsburg Landing

RM 215

Administration Site

Silver Shed

Klopton Creek

Upper Pittsburg Landing

RM 216.3

Scenic River
Wild River

Fish Trap Bar

Corral Creek

Muir Creek

OREGON

IDAHO

Cat Gulch

Kirby Creek Resort

RM 220

Kirby Creek

Yankee Bar
Cougar Creek

Russell Bar

Slaughter Gulch

Kirkwood Bar

Kirkwood Historical Ranch

Two Corral

Lower Salt Creek

Upper Salt Creek

Half Moon Bar

Gracie Bar

Suicide Point

Temperence Creek

Buckman Ranch

Landing Strip

Dry Gulch

Big Bar

N

SNAKE RIVER
Temperence Creek
to
Pittsburg Landing
Mile 225 — 212

one mile

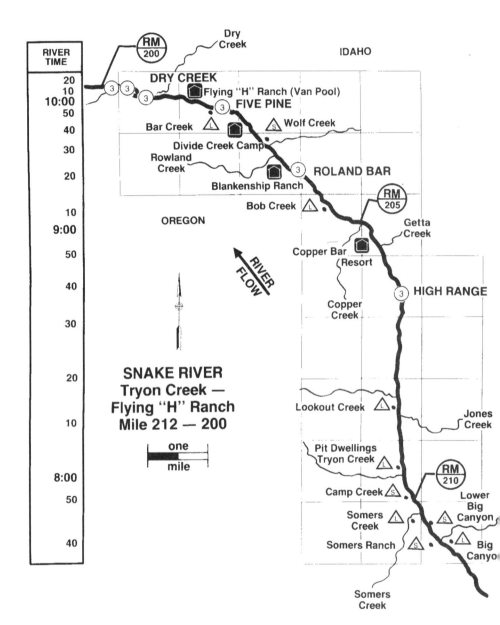

SNAKE RIVER
Tryon Creek —
Flying "H" Ranch
Mile 212 — 200

one mile

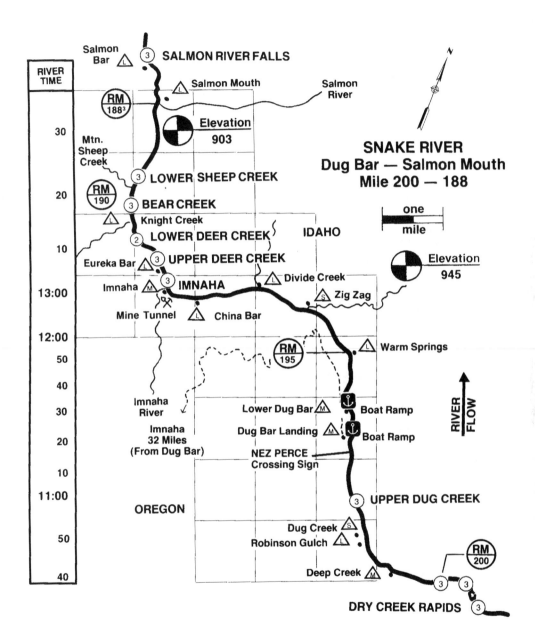

RIVER TIME

Salmon Bar

③ SALMON RIVER FALLS

△ Salmon Mouth

Salmon River

RM 188³

Elevation 903

30

Mtn. Sheep Creek

③ LOWER SHEEP CREEK

20

RM 190

③ BEAR CREEK

△ Knight Creek

② LOWER DEER CREEK

IDAHO

10

Eureka Bar △ ③ UPPER DEER CREEK

Imnaha Ⓜ ③ IMNAHA

△ Divide Creek

Ⓢ Zig Zag

13:00

Mine Tunnel △ China Bar

12:00

RM 195

△ Warm Springs

50

40

Imnaha River

Lower Dug Bar Ⓜ ⚓ Boat Ramp

30

Imnaha 32 Miles (From Dug Bar)

Dug Bar Landing △Ⓜ ⚓ Boat Ramp

20

NEZ PERCE Crossing Sign

10

11:00

③ UPPER DUG CREEK

OREGON

50

Dug Creek Ⓢ

Robinson Gulch △

RM 200

40

Deep Creek Ⓜ

③ ③

DRY CREEK RAPIDS ③

SNAKE RIVER
Dug Bar — Salmon Mouth
Mile 200 — 188

one mile

Elevation 945

RIVER FLOW

123

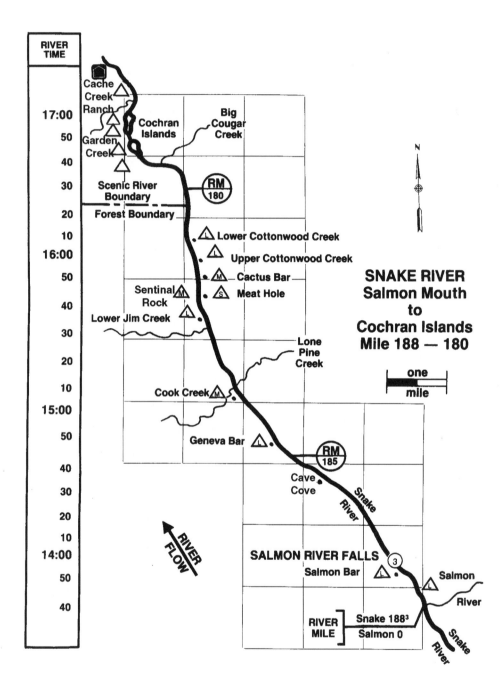

RIVER TIME

17:00
50
40
30
20
10
16:00
50
40
30
20
10
15:00
50
40
30
20
10
14:00
50
40

Cache Creek Ranch
Garden Creek
Cochran Islands
Big Cougar Creek
Scenic River Boundary
Forest Boundary
RM 180
Lower Cottonwood Creek
Upper Cottonwood Creek
Cactus Bar
Sentinal Rock
Meat Hole
Lower Jim Creek
Lone Pine Creek
Cook Creek
Geneva Bar
RM 185
Cave Cove

RIVER FLOW

SALMON RIVER FALLS
Salmon Bar
Salmon

Snake River

Salmon River

SNAKE RIVER
Salmon Mouth
to
Cochran Islands
Mile 188 — 180

one mile

N

RIVER MILE
Snake 188³
Salmon 0

Snake River

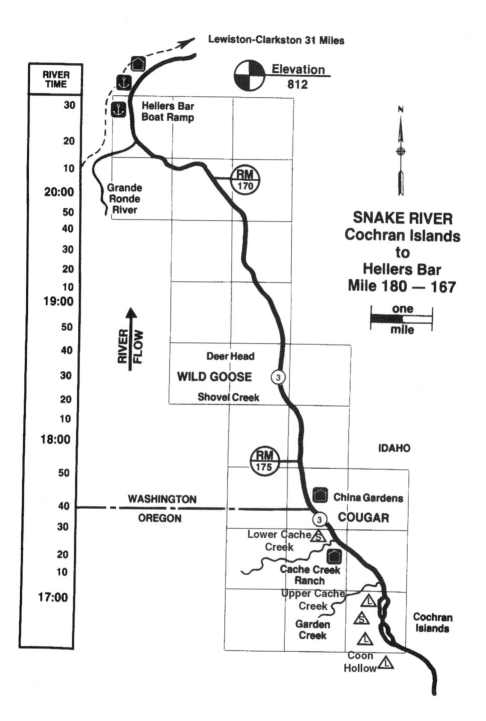

Lewiston-Clarkston 31 Miles

Elevation
812

SNAKE RIVER
Cochran Islands
to
Hellers Bar
Mile 180 — 167

one
mile

N

RIVER TIME	
30	
20	
10	
20:00	
50	
40	
30	
20	
10	
19:00	
50	
40	
30	
20	
10	
18:00	
50	
40	
30	
20	
10	
17:00	

Hellers Bar
Boat Ramp

RM 170

Grande
Ronde
River

RIVER FLOW

Deer Head

WILD GOOSE   ③

Shovel Creek

RM 175

IDAHO

China Gardens

WASHINGTON

OREGON

③ COUGAR

Lower Cache
Creek

Cache Creek
Ranch

Upper Cache
Creek

Garden
Creek

Cochran
Islands

Coon
Hollow

References

1. *Oregon River Tours* by Garren — includes Hells Canyon

2. *Floating the Wild Selway* — West Fork Ranger District
   6735 West Fork Road
   Darby, MT 59829

3. *The Middle Fork of the Salmon* — Middle Fork Ranger District
   Challis National Forest
   Challis, ID 83226

4. *The Salmon — A Wild and Scenic River*
   North Fork Ranger District
   Salmon National Forest
   North Fork, ID 83466

5. *Lower Salmon River Guide* —
   U.S. Bureau of Land Management
   Route 3 Box 181
   Cottonwood, ID 83522

6. *The Wild and Scenic Snake River Boater's Guide*
   Hells Canyon National Recreation Area
   P.O. Box 699
   Clarkston, WA 99403

7. *Handbook of the Middle Fork of the Salmon River* by Quinn

8. *The Big Drops* by Collins and Nash

9. *Idaho Whitewater* by Moore and McClaren

10. *Idaho the Whitewater State* by Amaral

11. *An Innocent on the Middle Fork* by DuBois

12. *The Middle Fork and the Sheepeater War*
    by Carrey and Conley

13. *River of No Return* by Carrey and Conley

14. *Snake River of Hells Canyon* by Carrey and Conley

15. *Middle Fork of the Salmon River* by Leidecker